Narrowing the Achievement Gap in a (Re)Segregated Urban School District

Research, Practice, and Policy

A volume in
The Achievement Gap: Research, Policy, and Practice
C. Kent McGuire and Vivian W. Ikpa, *Series Editors*

Narrowing the Achievement Gap in a (Re)Segregated Urban School District

Research, Practice, and Policy

Vivian W. Ikpa

C. Kent McGuire
Temple University

INFORMATION AGE PUBLISHING, INC.
Charlotte, NC • www.infoagepub.com

Library of Congress Cataloging-in-Publication Data

Ikpa, Vivian W.
  Narrowing the achievement gap in a (re)segregated urban school district :
research, practice, and policy / Vivian W. Ikpa, C. Kent McGuire.
      p. cm. – (The achievement gap, research, practice, and policy)
  Includes bibliographical references.
  ISBN 978-1-60752-221-8 (pbk.) – ISBN 978-1-60752-222-5 (hardcover)
  1. African Americans–Education–Virginia–Norfolk. 2. Academic
achievement–Virginia–Norfolk. 3. Educational change–Virginia–Norfolk.
4. School integration–Virginia–Norfolk. 5. Norfolk (Va.)–Race
relations. I. McGuire, C. Kent. II. Title.
  LC2803.N67I46 2009
  371.829'960755521–dc22
                                                          2009025614

CONTENTS

ACKNOWLEDGMENTS

We acknowledge and support all children in our nation's public schools—they are our future.

Narrowing the Achievement Gap in a (Re)Segregated Urban School District, page xi
Copyright © 2009 by Information Age Publishing
All rights of reproduction in any form reserved.

SERIES EDITORS' PREFACE

The achievement gap may be defined as the disparity in academic performance between specific groups of students. These gaps are frequently observed when analyzing standardized test scores, grade point averages, dropout rates, and college enrollment. We believe that it is important to understand that these deficits are impacted by a confluence of structural and institutional factors, including; economic status, teacher quality, school funding, school governance models, demographic shifts, and other system inputs and through-puts. In narrowing performance gaps, these factors must be given appropriate attention. This book examines the achievement gap between minority subgroups and their non-minority counterparts and elaborates strategies utilized by the Norfolk City Public Schools Districts in narrowing academic achievement gaps. One unique feature of this book and others in this series is the emphasis on data-driven analyses of variables and factors directly related to student performance. Specifically, this volume explores issues directly related to: (1) how data can be used to inform practice and policy in addressing student performance; (2) how school leaders, parents, students, community leaders, policy makers and other related internal and external actors affect academic achievement; and (3) identifying successful strategies developed and implemented by urban school districts in narrowing achievement gaps. This book also elaborates the relationship between gaps in achievement and policy mandates the designed to promote accessibility to educational opportunities. Central to this book is the belief that policymakers at all levels must acknowledge that the achievement gap is influenced by global structural problems pervading our society; therefore, social, political and economic deficits are discussed

Narrowing the Achievement Gap in a (Re)Segregated Urban School District, pages xiii–xiv
Copyright © 2009 by Information Age Publishing
All rights of reproduction in any form reserved.

within this context. This book and others in this series should be of interest to students enrolled in courses in urban school leadership, policy studies, and foundations of education. Additionally, books in this series can be used in social policy, and education reform courses. Colleges of education throughout the United States, South Africa and the United Kingdom can broadly use this series. These countries are experiencing similar problems with achievement gaps, changing demographics, and education policy reform. The focus and organization of this book are presented in the Introduction, Chapter 1.

C. Kent McGuire
Vivian W. Ikpa

CHAPTER 1

INTRODUCTION

*Many say that only free people ought to be educated, but we should rather
believe the philosophers who say that only the educated are free.*
—Epictetus, Discourses, 101 AD

School desegregation has been a topic of debate among social scientists for more than a century. The judicial rationale for this policy resulted from the 1954 *Brown* decision in which the United States Supreme Court unanimously ruled that African American children should receive the same quality of education as their European American counterparts. In essence, the court declared the practice of segregating students in the public schools based upon race to be unconstitutional by declaring that de jure segregation violated the Equal Protection clause of the Fourteenth Amendment. The court mandated that school districts eliminate dual education and eliminate segregation in the nation's schools with all deliberate speed. The high court placed the primary responsibility for dismantling segregated schools on local boards of education. It should also be noted that by 1964, only one percent of all African American children in the south attended desegregated school (McAndrews, 1998). The courts recognized that if individual states were left to desegregate without federal oversight, desegregation would not become a reality. It was the Title IV of the Civil Rights Act of 1964 that allowed the United States Justice Department to litigate school desegregate school desegregation cases and Title VI gave the Department of Health Education and Welfare the authority to withhold funding to districts that refused to desegregate (McAndrews, 1998). Despite the ruling handed down by the United States Supreme Court in the 1955 *Brown II* decision, the state of Virginia and many

Narrowing the Achievement Gap in a (Re)Segregated Urban School District, pages 1–8
Copyright © 2009 by Information Age Publishing

1

other states throughout the south continued to operate separate schools for African Americans and their European American peers. Virginia has long been considered a politically conservative state with a history of embracing segregated schooling and separatism in its social institutions. Therefore, in response to the 1954 Supreme Court ruling in *Brown v. Topeka, Kansas Board of Education*, the state adopted and implemented legislation designed to keep state schools segregated. State funding was withheld from integrated school districts and Virginia's era of "Massive Resistance" to school desegregation was born. Rather than desegregate schools, several districts decided to close their schools. This massive resistance to the *Brown* decision became evident when Charlottesville, Norfolk, and Prince Edward County, Virginia closed their doors to avoid the desegregation mandate. This politically driven plan of massive resistance reflected the belief that a successful defense against desegregation was possible and desirable for the good of society and that segregated schooling should be continued. In 1956, African American parents in the city of Norfolk sued to integrate the public schools. These individuals recognized that social, academic and economic gaps resulted from segregated social institutions and found this undesirable. However, the city continued to resist school desegregation and the United States Supreme Court's mandates handed down in *Brown I* and *Brown II*, and the legal battles continued for sixteen additional years.

Although the United States Supreme Court ordered the public schools to desegregate, the Norfolk City Public Schools District did not desegregate until January 1970. In 1971, a federal judge approved a desegregation plan that required cross-town busing between paired schools. Almost 50 percent of the district's students were transported (bused) to new schools. Busing eliminated the racially identifiable, all-African-American schools in the district. At the time of Norfolk's 1970 public schools desegregation efforts, 57 percent of the system's 56,830 students were European-Americans and 43 percent were African-Americans. However, after more than fifteen years of mandated desegregation, enrollment dropped to 34,803 students, and the members of the local school board voted to abolish cross-town busing for desegregation at the elementary school level. The board submitted a revised desegregation plan that assigned students to neighborhood schools, thereby creating ten elementary schools that were comprised of more than 95 percent African-American students. However, this new neighborhood school plan was challenged in the United States District Court for the Eastern District of Virginia. Although the court originally ordered the district to desegregate, it withdrew from the case in 1975 and ruled that the Norfolk City Public Schools District were unitary. Although the district had obtained unitary status, the plaintiffs contended that the system had become more segregated since 1975 and that student performance would be adversely affected in resegregated schools. Unfortunately, the district court did not agree with the plaintiffs, and, in 1986, the Norfolk School Board presented to the United States District Court for the Eastern District of Virginia a resolution for review and approval of adopting a neighborhood school. This divided the city's thirty-seven elementary schools into three categories: (a) ten resegregated schools comprising over 95 percent African-American enrollment, (b) racially mixed schools comprising 10 to 50 percent European-American enrollment, and (c) predominately European-American schools comprising over 50 percent European-American enrollment.

Many sociopolitical changes have occurred since the 1954 *Brown* decision, and the world is not the same. It is time to realize that there is little support for school desegregation and, in many instances, it is difficult to find majority students in urban school districts; therefore, racial desegregation is not a viable reality. We need to understand that it is time to move beyond *Brown* because demographic changes have extended the *Brown* debate beyond the United States' borders. This is not the 1950s or 1960s; therefore, resegregation must be viewed within the context of global economies and political shifts that continue to bring cultural, racial/ethnic, and economic diversities into the nation's public schools. Given this contention, it is time to reframe the education policy/school reform debate to reflect the global reality that we must focus attention on variables that have been proven to be successful in improving student performance.

We should also realize that the courts have handed down decisions that served to facilitate school resegregation; however, other factors have also affected the return to segregated neighborhood schools. It is apparent that the nation's schools have become more segregated as a result of the convergence of global economic shifts, housing patterns, court decisions, demographic changes, and the perception that public schools do not give children the competitive edge needed to function in a global, technology driven society.

Patterns of immigration have also increased the levels of diversity in urban centers. In fact, many families have fled urban communities because of decaying infrastructures, inferior schools, violence, and substandard living conditions. These changes have resulted in de facto segregation and the resegregation of public schools. The United States Supreme Court ruled in *Milliken v. Bradley* (1974) that urban-suburban desegregation plans could not be implemented by school districts without evidence that suburban school districts engaged in de jure segregation designed to maintain segregated schools. Perhaps social and public policy mandates should examine, propose, and implement strategies that will desegregate other social institutions so that authentic desegregation will become evident. Mandated public school desegregation is (or was) artificial. If students spend six hours a day in forced desegregated (not integrated) educational settings that have no connections to their community or other life experiences, this will frequently result in cultural disconnects and academic deficits.

In 2009, as school districts throughout the nation continue to resegregate, we still hear the voices of those supporting school desegregation efforts, and their cries must not be silenced. The battle for equality has not ended and all should remember that the 1980s reflected a political ideology from the federal court and the Reagan Administration that school desegregation mandates would no longer be enforced. The United States Supreme Court facilitated the dismantling of school desegregation plans by public school districts. Another legal blow to school desegregation became apparent in the high court's 1991 ruling in *Board of Education of Oklahoma City v. Dowell.* In this decision, the United States Supreme Court ruled that school districts could be released from court supervision once all vestiges of school desegregation "to the extent practicable" were addressed. The court further defined "practicable" in its 1992 ruling in *Freeman v. Pitts*, which stated that as long as school districts can show a "good will faith," these districts can be declared unitary before full compliance has been achieved in every area of school operations. As one can see, during the 1990s, the school desegregation debate shifted from *de jure* to *de facto.* The road to resegregation became less bumpy with this ruling as the nation's schools abandoned desegregation plans. As Orfield and Lee (2007), noted:

> National statistics for black students show very slow progress for the first decade after *Brown,* then a subsequent decline in black segregation from whites from the mid-1960 through the early 1970s. There was gradual improvement through most of the 1980s, but then a reversal and steady gradual rise in segregation since the early 1990s a rise that is accelerating in the south. . . . There has been a steady rise in the percentage of black students in majority schools since the 1980s and by far the largest increase in the south. (p. 28)

As we approach the end of the first decade of the twenty-first century, the Norfolk School District continues to exist as a (re)segregated educational system. It is essential that policymakers, educators and other stakeholders consider the impact of attending segregated schools on the achievement gap between minority groups and European-American students attending the resegregated public schools in the city of Norfolk. Although integrated public schools are becoming increasingly more difficult to find, social scientists should continue to investigate the relationship between attending integrated school attendance and the achievement gap between African Americans and their European American counterparts.

A CHALLENGE TO EDUCATORS

The interplay between sociopolitical forces and economic agendas becomes apparent when one examines the June 28, 2007 United States Supreme

Court decision, *Parents Involved in Community Schools v. Seattle School District.* In a reversal of the 1954 *Brown* decision, the Supreme Court ruled that public schools could not use race as a factor when assigning children to public schools. Given demographic shifts, globalization, economic instability, and ideological shifts, the reversal was expected. However, it is essential that policymakers, educators, and other stakeholders consider the impact of segregated school attendance on the achievement gap that continues to exist between minority groups and European Americans attending resegregated neighborhood schools.

FOCUS OF THE BOOK

This book will focus on the test score gaps between African American and European American students. The achievement gaps between these two groups will be analyzed and elaborated. Additionally, the authors will analyze how changes in such school characteristics as racial composition, school composition, school expenditures, and socioeconomic levels of neighborhoods affect achievement-gap trends in the Norfolk School District. An examination of these trends in an urban school district will serve to better inform public policy and school reform efforts.

NORFOLK CITY PUBLIC SCHOOLS: A MODEL RESEGREGATED URBAN DISTRICT

On Tuesday, September 20, 2005, the Norfolk Public School District was awarded the Broad Prize for urban education. This prestigious award is given to the urban school district that has made the most progress in narrowing achievement gaps among ethnic minorities as well as among economically stratified students. According to the Broad Foundation (2008), its mission is "to improve K–12 urban public education through better governance, management, labor relations, and competition." Additionally, the organization seeks to:

> train a broad, deep bench of current and aspiring school leaders in education; redefine the traditional roles, practices and policies of school board members, superintendents, principals and labor union leaders to better address contemporary challenges in education; attract and retain the highest quality talent to leadership roles in education; equip school systems and their leaders with modern tools for effective management; provide tangible incentives for educators to advance academic performance; and honor and highlight success wherever it occurs in urban education. (Broad Foundation, 2008)

As mandated by the Broad Foundation, the Norfolk School District utilized their $500,000 award to fund scholarships for graduating seniors. The district was selected as one of five finalists each year between 2002 and 2005. Norfolk City Public School District Superintendent, Dr. Stephen Jones noted that the district strategically focused on "closing the gaps and increasing performance for all students." Although the district has narrowed racial and socioeconomic gaps, there is still much to accomplish. The district's academic disparities and structural gaps continue to be widely debated among social scientists and policymakers. Many contend that the gap in academic performance between African American and European American students is directly related to the intellectual inferiority of African Americans, cultural deficits, economic inequities, capitalistic domination, and societal structural problems. However, in an effort to better understand the dynamics involved in narrowing achievement gaps, perhaps one should focus on success stories such as Norfolk. Educators, researchers, and policymakers may need to rethink research findings based on deficits models that present minority students as pathological entities. In other words, we know what has not been successful—now let us focus on urban districts that are beating the odds and challenging the students in resegregated public school districts.

THE GOALS OF THIS BOOK

The specific goals of this book are to describe the achievement gap between minority African American students and European American students in the Norfolk School District and to present strategies utilized by urban districts to narrow the gap. One unique feature of this book is that it provides a data-driven, research-based analysis of the achievement gap between minority and European American students.

We must identify programs and practices that can improve student academic performance and make certain that these strategies survive in a politically charged, culturally dynamic world. As we end the first decade of the twentieth-first century, it is important to continue the quest for equality. *Roberts, Plessy, Brown,* and *Riddick* are cases that directly affected educational equality and equity in the city of Norfolk. One should also note that demographic shifts have resulted in changes in education policies at federal and state levels. The No Child Left Behind Act of 2001 (NCLB) requires careful state monitoring of achievement gaps and mandates the stratification of these performance gaps by socioeconomic background, racial and ethnic groups, language, and disability. The Obama Administration is in the process of extending and revising this policy in terms of more realistic accountability measures and hopefully, adequate resources to bring about change.

THE ORGANIZATION OF CHAPTERS

Chapters 1 and 2 provide an introductory overview of the research setting and discussions of challenges confronting twenty-first century urban districts and communities. They emphasize the point that the world has changed and that resegregated public schools exist due to demographic, political, and economic complexities. Attention is also given the plight of academic and economic gaps. The academic crisis among African American men is also elaborated.

Chapters 3 and 4 of this book detail the history of the legal battle for school desegregation and examine massive resistance policies in the state of Virginia. The story of the state's plan of avoiding *Brown I* and *Brown II* is analyzed against the sociopolitical conservatism enveloping the state and the region, as well as the growing Civil Rights Movement of the middle 1950s and 1960s. The changing faces of school desegregation and the achievement gap will be elaborated in terms of the racial isolation enveloping the city during the 1950s and 1960s. Additionally, we will examine the effects of mandated desegregation in the 1970s as well the legal retrenchment as related to academic achievement in the 1980s and 1990s.

Finally, a description of the racial/ethnic achievement gap in the Norfolk school district during the era of increasing resegregation (2000–2006) will be analyzed. Specific attention will be given to African American achievement gaps. As Harvard law professor Jay Heubert (1999), noted in *School Law Reform*, school desegregation gave minority students more opportunities in the 1960s and 1970s and lost ground in the 1980s and 1990s. This section of the book will build on Heubert's contentions in terms of analyzing gap data.

Chapter 5 presents and elaborates on the body of scholarly research related to desegregated schooling and the African American/European American achievement gaps.

Chapter 6 examines racial/ethnic achievement gaps between minority and European American children in the Norfolk public schools. This data-driven section is supported with graphs and tables to simplify and enhance discussions. Given the rapidity with which many school districts have abandoned desegregation plans in order to resegregate, one alarming finding indicated that as the percentages of European Americans increased in schools, the achievement gap between African Americans and European Americans decreased.

Chapter 7 presents a comparative analysis of the achievement-gap data relevant to subgroups. These data were be utilized to analyze achievement gaps by race, gender, and income level.

Chapter 8 provides a summary of successful strategies utilized by urban school districts to narrow achievement gaps. Specific policy implications will also are addressed. Additionally, appendices, tables, references and a subject index are included.

CHAPTER 2

URBAN CHALLENGES AND THE ACHIEVEMENT GAP

*Through education, society can formulate its own purposes, can organize
its own means and resources, and thus shape itself with definiteness and economy
in the direction in which it wishes to move. . . . Education thus conceived
marks the most perfect and intimate union of science and art
conceivable in human experience.*

—John Dewey, 1897

In this era of bailouts and stimulus incentives, schools and communities have been left to cope with a depressed economy as well as global social, political, and technological shifts. It is within this context that educators and social scientists seek to place, at center stage, the issues surrounding student achievement in the policy-making arena. One should examine these issues by revisiting the state of education in the nation's urban school districts. Many schools located in urban communities serve large numbers of children living at or below the poverty level. These schools, like many other social institutions are overburdened and severely underfunded. Frequently, these schools are characterized by overcrowded classrooms, outdated resources, and limited resources. Teachers often face day-to-day challenges that force them to develop and implement cost effective, creative survival techniques as they attempt to stimulate student to learn. As McGuire (2008) noted, in an effort to improve student achievement, those in leadership and decision-making positions must constantly address the complexities and challenges enveloping increasingly diverse and global urban communities. Additionally, McGuire (2008) contended that there are numerous structural features in funding systems that severely affect the school's ability to meet students' needs.

As we continue to witness the demise of many financial institutions and changes in family structure, we are reminded that policymakers and educators are confronted with financial challenges that affect measures of economic well-being and limit life chances of urban children. Unfortunately, politicians, community leaders, and other stakeholders are left to endure political battles that give rise to disjointed decisions that do little to solve the problems confronting the nation's schools. In response to global economic changes, school systems are seeking to develop efficiency-driven governance models based on corporate structures grounded in economic rationalism. It is apparent that external and internal sociopolitical forces driven by the economic models guiding capitalistic ideology will continue to reshape school governance and leadership both nationally and internationally. As President Obama stated in a speech delivered on March 11, 2009, to the United States Hispanic Chamber of Commerce:

> America will not remain true to its highest ideals—and America's place as a global economic leader will be put at risk—unless we not only bring down the crushing cost of health care and transform the way we use energy, but also if we do—if we don't do a far better job than we've been doing of educating our sons and daughters; unless we give them the knowledge and skills they need in this new and changing world. For we know that economic progress and educational achievement have always gone hand in hand in America. . . . The source of America's prosperity has never been merely how ably we accumulate wealth, but how well we educate our people. This has never been more apparent than it is today. In a twenty-first century world where jobs can be shipped wherever there's an Internet connection, where a child born in Dallas is now competing with a child in New Delhi, where your best job qualification is not what you do, but what you know—education is no longer just a pathway to opportunity and success, it is a prerequisite for success. (Obama, 2009)

As the new president unveils his education reform plan, it is important for all of us to review the status of academic achievement in our nation's schools. As a nation, we cannot allow our disadvantaged children to continue to be undereducated in poorly conceived, poorly staffed, and poorly governed, and underfunded public schools. It is morally wrong and economically unsound to focus solely on the economy at the expense of education. If we can bail out banks, automobile companies, major corporations, and the next-door neighbor, we can also provide a stimulus incentive for our failing urban schools.

Analysis of data indicated that, in 2003, only 55% of the nation's African American students graduated from high school on time as compared to

78% of their European American counterparts (Greene & Winters, 2005). Additionally, on the average, African American and Hispanic students in grade twelve read at about the same level as European American eighth graders (U.S. Department of Education, Office of Vocational and Adult Education, 2002). Further examination of data indicated that about 50% of poor, urban students in grade nine read only at a fifth or sixth grade level (Neild & Balfanz, 2001). It is also disturbing to note that in 2005, 89% of African American eighth grade students read below grade level as compared to 63% of their European American peers (U.S. Department of Education, NCES, 2005). The performance of African American males lags below all other subgroups.

Analysis of data indicated that the grade twelve reading scores of African American males were lower than those of their male and female counterparts across all other racial and ethnic groups (U.S. Department of Education, NCES, 2005).

BEATING THE ODDS—WILL OUR CHILDREN WIN?

A review of population trends indicated that more than 60% of all African American students attend schools in their neighborhoods and 50% of their peers are living in poverty as compared to 18% of European American students (Orfield & Lee, 2005). It is also important to note that the nation's public schools are approximately 41% non-European American and that the majority of minority group children attend schools that have a high segregation index (Orfield & Lee, 2005). Findings also suggested that high-poverty schools, where the majority of the population is comprised of minorities, are five times more likely not to graduate high school students on time than majority European American schools (Balfanz & Legters 2004). It has also been documented that in thirty-one states, school districts with the largest number of minority students receive fewer resources than those districts with the smallest number of minority students (Carey, 2004). Students attending high schools where 75% or more of the students are at a low socioeconoimic level are three times as likely to be taught by uncertified teachers who are teaching English and Science than those schools attended by more affluent students (Wirt et al., 2004). Data also revealed that 29% of African American students attended schools with decaying and dirty physical facilities as compared to 18% of European American students.

Other indicators of included graffiti: 10% for African American students vs. 3% for their European American peers. Additionally, the same conditions were found in examining the ceilings in the schools; 12% African American students as compared to 7% European American students (Planty & Devoe 2005). The Council of the Great City Schools collected data on the achievement of students in selected city public school districts. Findings from their research indicated that scores have improved in reading and mathematics on state tests and the National Assessment of Educational Progress, 2008. The Council examined achievement test scores of sixty-six urban school districts and the District of Columbia. The results indicated that the performance of fourth and eighth grade students in mathematics and reading increased between 2003 and 2004. These findings were published by the Council of the Great City Schools in "Beating the Odds: An Analysis of Student Performance and Achievement Gaps on State Assessment" (2008). Data from this report indicated that in 2006–2007, 63% of grade four urban school students scored at or above the proficiency level in mathematics, a 14-point increase from 2003. Eight graders also showed an increase in mathematics performance. In this group, 55% of the students were at or above the proficiency level in 2007, as compared to 49% in 2003. This 13-percentage point growth was significant. It is also interesting to note that the percentage of grade four urban school students scoring at or above the proficiency level increased from 51% in 2003 to 60% in 2007. During this same period, the percentage of eight graders performing at or above proficiency level increased from 43% in 2003 to 51% in 2007.

An analysis of performance trends on national assessments indicated that students attending major city public schools showed faster growth rates in mathematics and reading than the national group as measured by the NAEP. Findings indicated that, in 2007, approximately 28% of urban fourth graders scored at or above the proficiency level in mathematics on NAEP. This reflected an 8% gain from 2003 to 2007. The results suggested that 22% of the urban students in grade four scored at or above the proficient level in reading in 2007 as compared to 17% in 2003 (Council of Great City Schools, 2008). Data from the report's eighth annual analysis show that, in 2007, 22% of urban school districts now score as high as or higher than their respective states in fourth-grade math, and 16% score as high or higher at the eighth grade level.

Findings from the National Center for Education Statistics (2008), an annual report mandated by Congress, indicate that enrollment in the nation's public school has reached an all-time high and that schools are becoming more diverse. The percentage of European American students attending elementary and secondary public schools decreased significantly between 1986 and 2005 (See Table 2.1). In 1986, 70.4% of the children attending the nation's public elementary and secondary schools were European Americans. In 2000, the percentage declined to 61.2 and to 57.1 in 2005. On the other hand, the Hispanic and African Americans populations continued to increase. Between 1986 and 2005, African Americans

TABLE 2.1 Percentage Distributions of Public Elementary and Secondary School Enrollment, by Race/Ethnicity: 1986–87 and 1992–2006

Fall of school year	White	Total minority	Black	Hispanic	Asian/ Pacific Islander	American Indian/ Alaska Native
1986	70.4	29.6	16.1	9.9	2.8	0.9
1991	67.4	32.6	16.4	11.8	3.4	1.0
1993	66.1	34.0	16.6	12.7	3.6	1.1
1994	65.6	34.4	16.7	13.0	3.6	1.1
1995	64.8	35.1	16.8	13.5	3.7	1.1
1996	64.2	35.8	16.9	14.0	3.8	1.1
1997	63.5	36.5	17.0	14.4	3.9	1.2
1998	62.9	37.1	17.1	15.0	3.9	1.1
1999	62.1	37.9	17.2	15.6	4.0	1.2
2000	61.2	38.8	17.2	16.3	4.1	1.2
2001	60.3	39.7	17.2	17.1	4.2	1.2
2002	59.2	40.9	17.1	18.1	4.4	1.2
2003	58.7	41.3	17.2	18.5	4.4	1.2
2004	57.9	42.1	17.3	19.2	4.5	1.2
2005	57.1	42.9	17.2	19.8	4.6	1.2

Source: U.S. Department of Education, Office of Civil Rights, 1986 State Summaries of Elementary and Secondary School Civil Rights Survey, and National Center for Education Statistics, Common Core of Data (CCD), "Public Elementary/Secondary School Universe Survey, 1991–92 through 2005–06."

increased from 16.1% of the total enrollment to 17.2%. However, the fastest-growing group was Hispanics with a growth rate that has almost doubled in percentage since 1986. In 1986 Hispanic students comprised 9.9% of the total enrollment and by 2005, their enrollment increased to 19.8%. As McGuire (2008) noted, although students' test scores have improved overall in reading and mathematics for fourth and eighth graders, challenges for minority students continue to exist. The following indicators were reported:

> Total public school enrollment is projected to set new records each year from 2008 to 2017, at which time it is expected to reach 54.1 million.

> Minority students make up 43 percent of the public school enrollment overall and 48 percent in the South and 55 percent in the West.

Twenty percent of school-age children speak a language other than English at home, about 5 percent speak English with difficulty.

In 2005–06, about a third of Black students and a third of Hispanic students attended high-poverty schools compared with 4 percent of White students.

Between 1989–90 and 2004–05, total spending per student in public elementary and secondary schools rose 29 percent after adjusting for inflation, to $10,892.

Average reading scores of 4th and 8th graders were higher in 2007 than in 1992.

Average mathematics scores increased 27 points for 4th-graders and 19 points for 8th-graders between 1990 and 2007.

The dropout rates for Whites, Blacks, and Hispanics have generally declined between 1972 and 2006. Among public high school students in the class of 2005, about three-fourths graduated on time. (The Condition of Education, 2008)

It should also be noted that a careful analysis of data from NCES (2008) indicted that only 46% of grade four African American students were at or above basic performance in reading achievement (Table 2.2) as compared to 78% of European Americans students; 50% Hispanic students;

TABLE 2.2 Percentage Distribution of Students across Reading Achievement Levels, by Race/Ethnicity and Grade: 2007

Grade and level	Total	White	Black	Hispanic	Asian/ Pacific Islander	American Indian/ Alaska Native
4th grade						
Below basic	33	22	54	50	23	51
At or above basic	67	78	46	50	77	49
At or above proficient	33	43	14	17	46	18
At advanced	8	11	2	3	15	4
8th grade						
Below basic	26	16	45	42	20	44
At or above basic	74	84	55	58	80	56
At or above proficient	31	40	13	15	41	18
At advanced	3	4	#	1	5	2

Source: U.S. Department of Education, National Center for Education Statistics National Assessment of Educational Progress (NAEP), 2007 Reading Assessment and NAEP Data Explorer retrieved, March 1, 2009.

77% Asian/Pacific Islanders and 49% American Indian/Alaskan Native. Approximately 54% of African American fourth grade students scored below Basic levels on reading achievement. In grade eight, African American students continued to lag behind their peers. Again, 84% of the European American students scored at or above Basic performance in reading as compared with 55% African American; 58% Hispanic; 80% Asian/Pacific Islander; and 56% American Indian/Alaskan Native.

In mathematics, fourth grade African American groups underperformed all other subgroups. Thirty-six percent scored below basic levels performance on the achievement performance measure, as compared to 30% Hispanic and American Indian/Alaskan Native students, and 9% European American/Asian/Pacific Islander students (Table 2.3). By grade eight, the percent scoring below basic performance for all subgroups increased: 18% European American students, 53% African American students, 45% Hispanic students, 17% Asian Pacific Islander students, and 47% American Indian/Alaska native.

A review of science performance (Table 2.4) suggests that we are under-educating and mis-educating our African American and Hispanic students in the nation's public schools. In grade four, 62% of African American students are below Basic in science and only 38% are at or above basic performance on the science achievement measure. Hispanic students are also under-performing in grade four: 55% scored below Basic and only 45% performed at or above Basic. On the other hand, 82% of European American students

---

TABLE 2.3   Percentage Distribution of Students across Mathematics Achievement Levels, by Race/Ethnicity and Grade: 2007

Grade and level	Total	White	Black	Hispanic	Asian/ Pacific Islander	American Indian/ Alaska Native
4th grade						
Below basic	18	9	36	30	9	30
At or above basic	82	91	64	70	91	70
At or above proficient	39	51	15	22	58	25
At advanced	6	8	1	1	15	2
8th grade						
Below basic	29	18	53	45	17	47
At or above basic	71	82	47	55	83	53
At or above proficient	32	42	11	15	50	16
At advanced	7	9	1	2	16	2

Source: U.S. Department of Education, National Center for Education Statistics National Assessment of Educational Progress (NAEP), 2007 Mathematics Assessment, retrieved February 12, 2009 from http://nces.ed.gov/nationsreportcard/nde/.

TABLE 2.4 Percentage Distribution of Students across Science Achievement Levels, by Race/Ethnicity and Grade: 2005

Grade and level	Total	White	Black	Hispanic	Asian/ Pacific Islander	American Indian/ Alaska Native
4th grade						
Below basic	32	18	62	55	24	48
At or above basic	68	82	38	45	76	52
At or above proficient	29	40	8	11	36	14
At advanced	3	4	#	—	5	1
8th grade						
Below basic	41	26	72	65	34	66
At or above basic	59	74	28	35	66	34
At or above proficient	29	39	7	10	36	12
At advanced	3	5	#	#	6	1
12th grade						
Below basic	46	35	81	70	40	52
At or above basic	54	65	19	30	60	48
At or above proficient	18	24	2	5	23	13
At advanced	2	3	#	1	3	#

Source: U.S. Department of Education, National Center for Education Statistics National Assessment of Educational Progress (NAEP), Retrieved January 1, 2009 from http://nces.ed.gov/nationsreportcard/nde/.

performed at or above Basic in grade four and only 18% scored below Basic This bleak reality continued into grade eight for African American and Hispanic: 72% and 65% below grade level respectively. The grim reality appears to take center stage by grade twelve. At this point, the statistics are shocking in that 81% of African American and 70% of Hispanic students are performing below Basic in science as compare to 35% European American students, 40% Asian/Pacific Islander students, and 52% American Indian/Alaska Native students. These gaps have become craters!

Findings from Beating the Odds-VIII also indicated that racial/ethnic achievement gaps among students in urban school also narrowed between 2003 and 2007. Analysis of data found that:

Schools narrowed in math between 2003 and 2007, although they remain wide.

Some 66 percent of big city school districts narrowed the gap between their fourth-grade African-American students and white counterparts statewide in math proficiency—63 percent in eighth-grade math.

Among Hispanic students, 63 percent of the urban school districts narrowed the gap in math. In reading, between 2003 and 2007, 64 percent of major city school systems narrowed the achievement gap between fourth-grade African-American students and White counterparts statewide in reading proficiency 67 percent at the eighth-grade level.

Among Hispanic students, 57percent of urban school districts narrowed the gap with white fourth graders statewide—63 percent in eighth grade. (pp. 10–14)

An analysis of the primary grade level indicated that in 2004, minority groups comprised 42% of the total public school population in grades pre-kindergarten through second (NCES, 2007a). Additionally, data show that African American and Hispanic children are more likely to attend high-poverty schools than European American students. As we examine achievement, it becomes apparent that the academic performance of special populations in urban communities is not being adequately addressed. Findings from the 2005 National Assessment of Educational Progress revealed that fourth and eighth grade Asian/Pacific Islanders and European American students scored statistically significantly higher percentages on reading achievement tests than their African American and Hispanic peers. Results also indicated that Asian American/Pacific Islander students outperformed all other groups in mathematics. It is also interesting to note that in 2003, a significantly higher percentage of African American students in the elementary and secondary grade levels were expelled from school than their Hispanic, European American, Native American, and Asian/Pacific Islander counterparts.

Data from the National Center for Education Statistics (2007) indicated that:

Black, Hispanics, and American Indian/Alaskan Native American students are more likely to be eligible for free and reduced price lunch programs (frequently used as a measure of income level) than their White and Asian/Pacific Islander peers. Black and Hispanic students were also the most likely to attend high poverty schools, while Asian/Pacific Islander students were the most likely to attend low poverty schools. (p. 23)

It is also significant to note that:

31% of all students in the United States are concentrated in 1.5% of urban schools with total per person revenues that are only 89% of the average total pupil revenue.

Underfunding of urban schools is affected by funding formulas, including low weights for compensatory education, bilingual or English as a second language programs, and attendance-based foundation.

Urban schools enroll higher rates of immigrants and diverse students including ethnic, racial, linguistic, and religious populations.

Urban school enrollments are made up of 25% or more students who are low income.

Urban students are likely to have higher rates of mobility, absenteeism, and poor health. They are also less likely to have health coverage, which decreases attendance and reduces funding based on attendance-based formula. (p. 30)

THE ECONOMIC GAP

Data from the United States Census indicated that childhood poverty increased significantly between 1999 and 2004. The Poverty, Work and Opportunity Task Force (2007), chaired by Los Angeles Mayor Antonio R. Villaraigosa, was formed in January 2006 to respond to the structural conditions that give rise to the high poverty rates in the United States. Although extreme poverty envelopes urban landscapes, we must remember: poverty in America is not a racial or a regional issue. Thirty percent of all those identified as poor by federal statistics are White, 27% are African American, 21% are foreign-born Latinos and 8% are U.S.-born Latinos.

A review of data from the United States Department of Commerce (1990 and 2000); Census Bureau, Decennial Census, (1990 and 2000) and Factfinder, American Survey, (2008) indicated that although the percentage of Hispanic and African American family households living in poverty between 1899 and 2006 has decreased, African Americans and Hispanics have the highest percentage of children under 18 living at the poverty level (Table 2.5). In 2006, 28.7% of the African American families with school-age children were living in poverty: approximately 8.6% of married African American couples were at this level; 25.7% of the male-headed households and 43.5% of female households with no spouse present were at the poverty level. These statistics are also reflected among Hispanic families: 24.1% of the total households are at the poverty level; 15.6% of married Hispanic couples with school-age children also live in poverty. Male-headed Hispanic families had a 21.2% poverty rate, and homes headed by Hispanic females were at a 45.5% poverty level. European American total households indicated a poverty level of 11.4%; married couples, 5.3%; male-headed households, 15.1% and female-headed households 36.9%.

It is more important to debunk the popular misconception that somehow only urban centers are subject to "poverty." Rural areas are actually the most poor in the nation, as Fresno (CA) Mayor Alan Autry noted when he pointed out that the San Joaquin Valley in California has the highest concentration of poverty in the nation (Swann & Dyuduk, 2006, p. 1).

TABLE 2.5 Percentage of Family Households with Children Under 18 Living in Poverty, by Family Status and Race/Ethnicity: 1989, 1999, 2003, and 2006

Race/ethnicity	Total family households	Married couple	Male householder, no spouse present	Female householder, no spouse present
1989				
Total	17.6	7.3	19.5	42.3
White	10.5	5.9	15.6	34.3
Black	33.0	12.2	27.6	52.5
Hispanic	27.4	18.2	28.3	54.7
Asian/Pacific Islander	13.9	10.7	19.9	35.6
American Indian/Alaska Native	33.4	20.6	39.4	57.6
1999				
Total	13.6	6.6	17.7	34.3
White	9.4	5.0	14.3	27.8
Black	27.2	9.4	24.9	41.8
Hispanic	24.1	17.0	24.9	44.5
Asian/Pacific Islander	11.7	9.1	17.5	28.5
American Indian/Alaska Native	27.0	15.5	30.3	45.7
2003				
Total	14.9	6.6	18.0	36.5
White	11.5	5.7	15.4	32.2
Black	28.7	8.6	24.8	42.6
Hispanic	23.5	15.9	15.6	46.3
Asian/Pacific Islander	11.1	8.0	18.4	28.3
American Indian/Alaska Native	26.9	13.7	21.8	48.0
2006				
Total	15.0	6.5	17.7	36.9
White	11.4	5.3	15.1	32.4
Black	28.7	8.6	25.7	43.0
Hispanic	24.1	15.6	21.2	45.5
Asian/Pacific Islander	9.7	7.1	14.0	25.5
American Indian/Alaska Native	29.8	15.8	32.0	48.0

Source: U.S. Department of Commerce, Census Bureau, Decennial Census, 1990 and 2000; American Factfinder, American Community Survey.

Findings from a 19-city Mayors Hunger and Homelessness Survey (2007) conducted by the U.S. Conference of Mayors, indicated that high housing costs and the lack of affordable housing were linked to homelessness and hunger in families with children. The major findings from the survey indicated that the following structural problems are linked to increased poverty levels:

> The primary causes of hunger are poverty, unemployment, and high housing costs.
>
> The hunger crisis is fueled by the recent trends in foreclosures, the increased cost of living in general, and increased cost of food.
>
> The most common cause of homelessness among households with children is the lack of affordable housing.
>
> Among households with children, other common causes of homelessness are poverty and domestic violence. Among single individuals, the most common causes are mental illness and substance abuse.
>
> During the last year, members of households with children made up 23% of persons using emergency shelter and transitional housing programs in survey cities, while single individuals made up 76%. Only 1% of persons in these programs were unaccompanied youth. (p. 4)

THE AFRICAN AMERICAN MALE'S ACADEMIC CRISIS

In 2001, the Schott Foundation for public education funded a study on the achievement gap between male and female students attending K–12 schools. Findings indicated that female students were performing better than their male counterparts. The results regarding African American males showed that they performed lower than any other subgroup on achievement measures. As Holzman (2004) noted:

> The consequences of this widespread, deep, systemic failure to educate African American males are well known: high unemployment and imprisonment rates, little chance to attend and graduate from college, and unstable families.... states and districts with large African American enrollments can educate children, but do not educate most African American boys. (p. 3)

A review of relevant literature suggests that teachers who are able to provide culturally relevant strategies for African American males are likely to be successful (Love & Kruger, 2005).

It has also been found that teachers' values and beliefs about teaching impact academic performance and their students. These belief systems are shaped by life experiences and directly affect how they choices they make about their teaching strategies. These factors are directly linked to student achievement. (Britzman, 1998; Love & Kruger, 2005; Deemer, 2004). Ogbu's (1998) believes that "the treatment of minorities in the wider society is reflected in their treatment in education" (p. 159).

Although African American males comprise 33% of the total enrollment in the Norfolk City Public School District (See Tables 2.6 and 2.7), data from 2004 indicate that they are disproportionately represented in out-of-school suspension programs at 52.62%. European American males represent 14.84% of the total enrollment and 11.07% of out-of-school suspensions. A more extensive review of the data indicates that African American females comprise 33.075% of the total enrollment and 29.135% of suspensions, while European American females comprise 14.095% of the district's enrollment and account for only 4.85% of out-of-school suspensions. In terms of total expulsions, African American females and European American male each represent 20%. However, once again the African American male in the district is disproportionately represented in this category and accounts for 60% of total expulsions. On the other hand, no European American females were expelled from school during the 2000–2001 school

TABLE 2.6 Norfolk City Schools Students, African American Enrollment 2001–2002 by Gender

	Female African American	Female European American	Male African American	Male European American
Enrollment	11,785	5,020	11,950	5,290
Out of School Suspension	1,500	250	2,710	570
Total Expulsion	5	0	15	5
Total Mental Retardation	195	70	250	85
Emotional Disturbance	60	20	215	125
Specific Learning Disability	190	110	595	215

Source: Holzman (2004) Schott Inequity Index.

TABLE 2.7 Norfolk City Schools African American Enrollment by Student Percentage 2001–2002

	Female African American	Female European American	Male African American	Male European American
Enrollment	33.07	14.09	33.53	14.84
Out of School Suspension	29.13	4.85	52.62	11.07
Total Expulsion	20.00	0.00	60.00	20.00
Total Mental Retardation	31.71	11.38	40.65	13.82
Emotional Disturbance	14.12	4.71	50.59	29.41
Specific Learning Disability	16.59	9.61	51.97	18.78

Source: Holtzman (2004) Schott Inequity Index

year. The statistics become more revealing when one examines the percentage of African American males in special-education classes. Data suggest that 40.65% of all mentally retarded students in the Norfolk City Public School District are African American males; 31.5% are African American females; 13.82% are European American males; and 11.38% are European American females. An analysis of data also indicated that 50.59% of students labeled as emotionally disturbed in the district are African American males; 29.41% are European males; 14.12% African American female; and 4.71% European American female. African American males also represented 51.97% of the total special learning-disabled category. African American female students reflected 16.59%; European American males, 18.78% and European American females, 9.61%.

The Norfolk Public City Schools District implemented high stakes assessment measures known as Virginia's Standards of Learning (SOL).

These tests are given annually to students at the elementary, middle, and high school grade levels. Although, after the 1999–2000 academic school year, the district reduced the achievement gap among subgroups, it and began to focus attention on the performance of African American males and the existing achievement gaps among subgroups. During the 2005–2006 school year, the district's middle schools implemented the following strategies:

> special education inclusion model for reducing the size self contained mathematics classes; daily mathematics reviews and quizzes; writing across the curriculum and core content areas; consistent and collaborative grading; and team planning. (Bailey, 2008, p. 1)

In 2007–2008, the Virginia Beach Public Schools District (an affluent suburb bordering Norfolk) focused attention and resources on the achievement gaps between African America males and non-African American males in the districts. Nine objectives were identified, and teachers were required to develop plans and implement strategies to close the gap among African American males and other subgroups. In comparing 2006–2007 and 2007–2008 SOL reading and mathematics test scores, the results indicated that:

Reading
Grade 5: The gap narrowed by 4.9% (from 16.9% to 12.0%)
Grade 6: The gap narrowed by 0.9% (from 14.4% to 13.5%)
Grade 7: The gap narrowed by 1.5% (from 12.3% to 10.8%)
Grade 8: The gap narrowed by 4.6% (from 18.0% to 13.4%)
The End of Course Test at the High school level narrowed 3.4% (from 12.0% to 8.6%)

Mathematics
Grade 5: The gap narrowed by 2.5% (from 20.8% to 18.3%)
Grade 6: The gap narrowed by 0.9% (from 16.4% to 15.5%)
Grade 7: The gap narrowed by 3.8% (from 27.2% to 23.4%)
Grade 8: The gap narrowed by 2.6% (from 15.4% to 12.8%)
The End of Course Test at the High school level narrowed 1.8%
(from 13.0% to 11.2%)

The district also showed progress in the number of African American males who successfully completed an advanced course as compared to the number of African American males in grades 6–8 and 9–12 from 2006–2007 and 2007–2008:

English
Grade 6: The gap narrowed by 3.6% (from 16.8% to 20.4%)
Grade 7: The gap narrowed by 5.2% (from 13.1% to 18.3%)
Grade 8: The gap narrowed by 2.7% (from 12.1% to 14.8%)
High School level percentage increased 1.8% (from 10.8% to 11.6%)

Mathematics
Grade 6: The gap narrowed by 2.6% (from 20.3% to 22.9%)
Grade 7: The gap narrowed by 6.9% (from 15.1% to 22.0%)
Grade 8: The gap narrowed by 3.1% (from 13.0% to 16.1%)
High School level percentage points increased 0.3%
(from 9.8% to 10.1%)

Science
Grade 6: The gap narrowed by 2.2% (from 19.0% to 21.2%)
Grade 7: The gap narrowed by 7.3% (from 11.7% to 19.0%)
Grade 8: The gap narrowed by 2.1% (from 10.5% to 12.6%)
High School level percentage points increased 0.1%
(from 27.4% to 27.5%)

Foreign Languages
Grade 7: The gap narrowed by 3.3% (from 6.2% to 9.5%)
Grade 8: The gap narrowed by 1.6% (from 21.9% to 23.5%)
High School level percentage points increased 0.1%
(from 9.6% to 9.7%)
(Virginia Beach City Public Schools, November, 2008)

The Virginia Beach Public School Districts implemented the following strategies in narrowing the achievement gap between African males and their non-African American peers:

The Virginia Department of Instruction identified best practices as related to the academic performance of African American males. These specifics were utilized to develop instructional guides for teachers. The Virginia department of education conducted professional sessions so that teachers could discuss the progress of African American males and share successful strategies. Staff members received training in cultural competency. A K–12 Literacy Plan addressing student needs is being developed. Principals are required to monitor the progress of African American males on each assessment measure throughout the academic year. New programs and Interventions capped in were put in place at schools to address the needs of African American male students. These include mentoring programs, student clubs, and other support organizations. Staff members in the Office of Student Leadership contact all students listed as dropouts to encourage them to return to school. A guidance plan was created for fifth grade students to increase the number of African American students enrolled in Advanced Placement classes as they transition into middle school. (Virginia Beach City Public Schools, 2008)

FUNDING GAPS

The decline in revenue reserves in urban centers can be directly linked to declining sales tax, income tax, and tourism tax revenues. Additionally, budget deficits have led to reductions in state support to local governments, and officials are forced to deal with increased expenditures in wages, health care, and pensions. These demands have forced downsizing of the workforce, reduced budgets, limited capital investment, and depleted reserves (Pagano, 2003). School districts receive funding from three sources: local, state, and federal aid; however, the 1980s gave birth to an era of New Federalism, which continues to thrive in 2008. This "do more with less" era is characterized by decreases in federal aid to education and an increase in corporate interest and influence. During the Reagan and Bush I Administrations, federal funding of urban programs was reduced by almost 70% (Fahim, 2005).

The degree to which state aid has substituted for the void created by the loss of federal support has varied. Some states barely increased support while others initially increased support and then reduced it because of concerns over balancing their own budgets. As a result, cities are expected to do more with less (Fahim, 2005, p. 3).It is obvious that many cities are not adequately funded and that there is a need to address issues surrounding underfunded urban schools. As Odden, Goetz, and Picus (2007) noted, nontraditional resources can account for over half of the funding for schools in urban districts. Those who govern urban schools may need to consider the benefits of developing broader based corporate/local school district partnerships in addressing funding gaps. In order to secure funding, urban school district leaders must be able to understand and negotiate the dynamics of an increasingly conservative political economy as they develop relationships with potential donors. Chief executive officers from the business sector have become key players in education reform initiatives. These individuals have joined forces with civic leaders and governmental officials and have formed national task forces and commissions to address the fiscal challenges pervading the nation's urban schools. In 2007, corporate-driven partnerships with urban school districts continue to exist. As was the case in the early 1980s and 1990s, corporate media campaigns are frequently employed to show support for public education and selected school reform initiatives that reflect the interest of business organizations. During the last two decades, two distinctive forms of corporate influence and dominance grew rapidly. These two modes of corporate involvement—business roundtables and business education partnerships—were typically organized to allow the business community access to the public education and the decision making process. According to McGuire (1990), business roundtables (sometimes called task forces, leadership groups, forums or commissions) are typically organized for the purpose of bringing business community interests to bear on education programs and policy decisions (p. 108).

As McGuire (2008) asserted, urban children are capable of achieving academic excellence; however, many often need additional educational assistance and special programs. Unfortunately, many of these programs are quite expensive and additional financial support is needed. Although research on the relationship between school finance and student achievement is mixed, Chubb and Hanushek (1990) reviewed 377 finance studies examining the relationship between spending and academic achievement. The researchers reported that there was no strong systemic relationship between school expenditures and student performance. However, Hedges, Laine, and Greenwald (1994) reanalyzed the same data and reported that a $500 increase in average spending per student would increase achievement by 0.7 standard deviation, and this was found to be statistically significant. When disparities in school funding exist on top of disparities in family income, it becomes clearer why there are such profound gaps in achievement between students from poorer backgrounds and those from wealthier homes (p. 12).

CHAPTER 3

THE LEGAL BATTLE
TO DESEGREGATE
PUBLIC SCHOOLS

Prejudices, it is well known, are most difficult to eradicate from the heart
whose soil has never been loosened or fertilized by education; they grow there,
firm as weeds among rocks.
—Charlotte Bronte, 1847

When many individuals think about segregated schooling in the nation's schools, they are often drawn to the battle for school desegregation in the early 1950s. However, they should be reminded of the 1849 *Roberts* case, which established the doctrine of separate, but equal. This case validated segregated schooling and provided the legal rationale for the *Plessy* decision. More than a century ago, the United States Supreme Court declared in *Plessy v. Ferguson* that maintaining separate but equal facilities for African Americans and European Americans in interstate transportation was unconstitutional. The high court also declared that separating the two races did not violate the Equal Protection Clause of the Fourteenth Amendment. This 1896 "separate but equal doctrine" was applied to just about every facet of American life. The *Plessy v. Ferguson* decision was utilized to justify separating African American and European Americans in public schools.

As far back as 1890 national attention was the plight of African American children when, President Rutherford Hayes convened a conference in

---

Narrowing the Achievement Gap in a (Re)Segregated Urban School District, pages 27–40
Copyright © 2009 by Information Age Publishing

Lake Mohonk, New York to discuss the education status of African Americans. As the president noted:

> The Negro population of this country now numbers nearly 8,000,000, of whom 1,320,000 are voters. By the year 1900 it is estimated that they will be in the majority in eight States. Among the present Negro population there are 1,103,000 colored children of school age who do not attend school, purely because of the absence of schools. According to the census of 1880, there were in the sixteen old slave States 4,715,395 persons over ten years of age who could not read or write, 63 per cent, of them, or 2,961,371, being grown up men and women, far beyond the school age. (Mohonk Conference on the Negro Question, 1st, 1890)

Additional discussions stated that:

> The 1,103,000 boys and girls in the South now out of school were born free, and are deprived of all educational advantages. The number of children is increasing more rapidly than the facilities for education. These children will soon be voters, exerting for good or evil an influence upon the nation. They will be fathers and mothers, molding the character of children, and charged with the performance of social, religious, and moral duties. Unless they are elevated by religion and education, they will inevitably impart to the coming generation the same defects which slavery has bred in them and their parents. (Covert, 1890, pp 31–32)

The *Brown* decision sought to address the academic and social gaps addressed at the Mohonk conference in 1890. In this 1954 decision, the Supreme Court declared the "separate but equal" education for African Americans and European Americans to be unconstitutional. One day after this landmark decision was handed down, Thurgood Marshall contended that segregated schools would be eliminated by the end of the decade:

> In the south, the percentage of Black students enrolled in schools with 90–100% nonwhite enrollments fell from 100% in 1954 to 78% in 1968 and 25% by 1972. consistent with this decline, the comparable percentage for the country as a whole fell from 64% in 1968 to less than 34% in both 1980 and 1989 (Clotfelter et al., p. 1)

Unfortunately, when Supreme Court Justice Marshall died almost four decades later, the schools were still segregated. *Roberts, Plessy,* and *Brown* represent historical legal battles for social justice and equality. In the year 2009, the schools are still segregated and have, in many instances, resegregated. In 1954, only 10 percent of public school students were minority group members. Today the public school segregation index continues to grow. In the Legal Battle to Desegregate Public Schools 2000, it increased from 37.4% for the nation. Between 1991 and 2000, it increased in every geographical region in the country (Clotfelter, 2004, p. 56.) Since the mid-1970s, the American public schools have become more segregated and have regressed to a pre-*Brown* pattern of segregation (Orfield, 2009).

Today the public school segregation index continues to grow. Since the mid-1970s, the American public schools have become more segregated and have regressed to a pre-*Brown* pattern of segregation (Orfield, 2009).

One should note that resistance to desegregation is not new. The concept of racial separatism can be traced to 1619 with the arrival of slaves from African. The White landowners considered the African slaves intellectually inferior to their European American free counterparts. The introduction of slaves into American society stripped African Americans of their cultural traditions and portrayed them as less than capable individuals who should be separated from European Americans. By 1800, all states passed laws preventing the importation of slaves (Weinberg, 1977). Additionally, all slave states had passed laws making it illegal to educate African Americans. Although it was against the law to educate African Americans, a few schools were established to provide vocational education (Weinberg, 1977). It was the intention of many to keep African Americans physically separate and intellectually unequal; therefore, education was not considered appropriate.

It is believed that the doctrine of "separate but equal "originated in 1849, prior to the *Plessy* decision (Levy & Phillips, 1951). One of the earliest challenges to segregated schooling is rooted in an 18th-century African American community in Boston, Massachusetts. It was during the late 1700s that the parents of African American children requested segregated school for their children. After the American Revolution, the city of Boston developed the first urban school district in the nation (Schultz, 1973). The district established three writing schools and three reading schools for all children between the ages of 7 and 14. During this time, African American children were allowed to attend school with their European American counterparts (Cubberly, 1947). Although the schools were integrated, the parents of African American children contended that European American teachers and students were treating their children unfairly (Schultz 1973). As a result of what they contended was harsh and unfair treatment, parents of African American students requested that the city of Boston provide publicly funded separate educational facilities for their children (Schultz, 1973). In 1787 Prince Hall, delivered a petition on behalf of the African American parents to the Massachusetts Legislature. This petition requested that the Boston School Committee establish a separate school for African American children in the community (Aptheker, 1969). The Commonwealth rejected this petition; however, the African American parents continued their fight. In 1798, Elisha Sylvester established a school for African American children in the home of Prince Hall (Woodson, 1919). Two years later, in 1800, the

African American community requested funding from the Boston School Committee in order to support separate schools for their children. The committee refused to fund these separate schools; however, the members agreed to fund a private school established by African American parents. By 1830, a segregated school system for African American children was in place in the city of Boston (Schultz, 1973). Although the request for separate schools was granted, the parents of African American children were not content. They complained that these schools were inferior in every way to those attend by European American children. In essence, the separate schools were unequal (Schultz, 1973).

During the 1840s, the City established one grammar school and two primary schools specifically for African American children. In 1883, the Boston Committee conducted a study to examine the effectiveness and quality of education in the city's schools. The results of the study indicated that salaries of African American teachers were significantly less than those of their African American counterparts (Schultz, 1973). Not unlike many urban districts in 2010, the African American schools were also found to be underfunded and many courses offered in the European American schools did not exist at the African American schools (Schultz, 1973). This study also found that African American children were being deprived of the resources needed to achieve a quality education (Schultz, 1973).

In 1844, more than one hundred years prior to the *Brown* decision, Thomas Dalton, along with seventy of his neighbors, led a protest demanding that their children be allowed to attend European American schools in the district. Benjamin Roberts tried to enroll his five-year-old daughter, Sarah in an all European American primary school (Schultz, 1973). This African American child applied for admission to the elementary school close to her home because she had to walk. Sarah walked past five other schools each day before reaching her school. This school, located on Smith Court, was intended specifically for African American students. A Boston City Ordinance, passed in 1845, stated that any child unlawfully excluded from the city's public schools could sue the city for damages. With this in mind, Sarah's father petitioned the all-European American school closest to her home for admission. The school rejected the plaintiff's application and sent her case to the Boston School Committee. The committee reaffirmed the school's decision (*Roberts v. City of Boston*, 1849). Although the committee denied admission to Sarah, she did not let this stand in her way. Sarah's parents attempted to enroll her in the school designated for European Americans. She was again rejected. As a result of the school's actions, Sarah's father filed a suit claiming that the Boston School Committee had violated the Massachusetts statute, which stated that qualified children could not be excluded from public education. The trial court ruled in favor of the school district (*Roberts v. City of Boston*, 1849).

In response to this ruling, city reformers sued the city of Boston in the Massachusetts Supreme Court on behalf of an African American child, Sarah Roberts. In 1850, the Supreme Judicial Court ruled that the Boston School Committee had a right to maintain separate schools for African American and European American children (*Roberts v. City of Boston*, 1849).

The Massachusetts Supreme Court ruled that Sarah Roberts had not been excluded from public education: however, her father had denied her admission by refusing to send her to the designated African American school (Nolte, 1971). The parents of African American children did not give up and in 1855, the Massachusetts General Assembly passed a law making segregation illegal. It is sad to note that almost 160 years after this decision, the nation's public schools still remain separate and unequal.

We are also reminded that, prior to the end of the Civil War, there were no public education systems for African Americans in the South. It was during the Reconstruction Era that public schools for African Americans were established. The southern states did not mandate segregation of schools; however, only two states, South Carolina and Louisiana, had laws against segregated schools. Although these states forbade segregated schooling, it was generally the rule that African Americans and European Americans attended separate schools. As Kousser and McPherson (1982), noted, only the University of South Carolina and some elementary schools in Louisiana were desegregated. From 1880 to early 1900s, state laws known as Black Codes were enacted in the south to "keep the black man in his place," Barth, (1974, p.26). These codes were put in place by southern states to limit the rights of freed slaves:

> The black codes lent sanction of the law to a racial ostracism that extended to churches and schools, to housing and jobs, to eating and drinking. Whether by law or custom, that ostracism eventually extended to virtually all forms of public transportation, to sports and recreation, to hospitals, orphanages, prisons, and asylums, and ultimately to funeral homes, morgues and cemeteries. (Woodward, 1966, p. 7)

From 1865 to 1935, school desegregation polices were challenged thirty-seven times; however, only nine were successful. In each of these thirty-seven cases, the doctrine of separate but equal was upheld by the court (Bardolph, 1970). The legal support for segregated schooling became evident in 1899 in *Cummings v. Board of Education*. In this case, a school board in the state of Georgia decided to close a public high school and convert it to an elementary school for African American students. Converting the high school to an elementary school left the African American students without a high school. The court decided that the fact that European American students were able to attend high school while their African American counterparts were left without a high school did not violate the

Equal Protection Clause of the Fourteenth Amendment. Justice Harlan decided that closing the all European American high school would only deprive European American students of an education and not help the African American students.

The doctrine of "separate but equal" was once again challenged in the 1896 case of *Plessy v. Ferguson*. In 1890, the state of Louisiana enacted a statute that maintained the separation of individuals by race in all railway transportation. During this era of separatism, the law stipulated that all railroads must provide *separate and equal* accommodations for African Americans and European American passengers. The law further stated that any individual found in violation of this law would be considered a criminal. One of the earliest challenges to this legal doctrine became apparent when Homer Adolph Plessy, a thirty-four year old "colored" man, purchased a first-class ticket from New Orleans to Covington, Louisiana. Unlike the framers of the law, Plessy realized that race is both a sociological and biological construct. That is, society labeled him as a colored while he was biologically, neither colored nor white. Plessy described himself as having seven-eighths Caucasian and one-eighth African blood and therefore, he contended that the law did not specifically apply to him.

On June 7, 1894, Plessy decided to sit in a section reserved for *white* passengers. The conductor asked Plessy to move to the section reserved for *colored* passengers; however, he refused. Plessy contended that he had the right to sit in the white section because he was seven-eighths white. As a result of his refusal to move to the colored section, Plessy was removed from the train and jailed in New Orleans (Rotunda, 1993). His attorney tried to have the charges declared unconstitutional on the grounds that Louisiana's *separate but equal* statute violated the constitutional right to equal protection of the law; however, Judge John H. Ferguson ruled against Plessy, and the Supreme Court upheld Louisiana's 1890 railway law. The law stated:

> All railway companies carrying passengers in their coaches in this state shall provide equal but separate accommodations. No person or persons shall be permitted to occupy seats in coaches, other than ones assigned to them on account of the race they belong to. (Barth, 1974, p. 30)

The Supreme Court ruled that separate facilities did not constitute *unequal* treatment and therefore did not violate the Fourteenth Amendment. The ruling held that as long as the facilities and opportunities provided African Americans and Whites were similar, the Equal Protection Clause was not violated (Rotunda, 1993.) The court also stated that providing separate facilities for African-Americans and European Americans did not necessarily infer the inferiority of either race. Justice Harlan wrote the dissenting opinion that offered a different perspective of the era. He stated:

> The thin disguise of equal accommodations will not mislead anyone, nor atone for wrongs this day done. Everyone knows that the statute in question had its origins in the purpose, not such much as to exclude white persons from railroad cars occupied by Negroes, as to exclude colored people from coaches occupied or assigned to white persons. Railroad corporations in Louisiana did not make discrimination among whites in the matter of accommodations for travelers. The thing to accomplish was under the guise of giving equal accommodations for Negroes and whites, to compel the later to keep to themselves while traveling in railroad passenger coaches.... The fundamental objection therefore, to the statute is that it interferes with the personal freedom of citizens.... If a white man and a Negro choose to occupy the same public conveyance on a public highway, it is their right to do so, and no government alone on the grounds of race can prevent it without infringing the personal liberty of each. (*Plessy v. Ferguson*, 163 U.S. 537, 1896)

It is apparent that the state of Louisiana did not adequately address or apply the "separate but equal" standard in the *Plessy v. Ferguson* decision. However, it should be noted that in this 1896 landmark ruling, the emphasis was on separate at the expense of equal. This became even more apparent in *Cummings v. Board of Education* (1899).

SEPARATE AND UNEQUAL IN HIGHER EDUCATION

The concept of separate but equal continued to flourish in society until the National Association for the Advancement of Colored People (NAACP) decided in the 1930s and 1940s to challenge the equality and equity of separate facilities for African Americans and European Americans in the nation's postsecondary institutions. The Equal Protection Clause of the Fourteenth Amendment clearly states: *"nor shall any state deprive any person within the jurisdiction the equal protection of the law"*. The intended purpose of this amendment was to enforce the equality of African-Americans and whites before the law (Epstein & Walker, 1995). During the twenty years prior to the *Brown* decision, other cases challenging the doctrine of separate but equal were argued before the Supreme Court. These cases were based on the contention that the doctrine of "separate but equal" violated the equal protection clause of the 14th Amendment.

The Supreme Court ruled in several higher-education cases that the *separate but equal* doctrine violated the equal protection clause of the Fourteenth Amendment. These post-secondary cases directly influenced the 1954 *Brown* decision. One of the most significant challenges to this doctrine is reflected in the case of *Gaines ex rel Missouri v. Canada*. In 1938, Lloyd Gaines applied to law school at the University of Missouri; however he was rejected for admission because he was African American. In keeping with the application of the separate but equal doctrine, university officials told him that he would have to attend a law school outside the state because Missouri did not have a separate law school for African American students. Gaines sought a writ of mandamus to gain admission to the university; however, the state court rejected his petition and the Supreme Court ruled that Gaines had a legal right to attend law school in the state of Missouri. The court further stated that since there were no separate law schools in the state for African Americans, he had the right to attend the white law school (*Gaines ex rel Missouri v. Canada*). The decision rendered in the *Gaines* case gave new meaning to the doctrine of separate but equal. Unlike the ruling in *Plessy*, the court emphasized *equal not just separate*. Chief Justice Hughes wrote:

> That for one intending to practice in Missouri there are special advantages in attending law school there, both in relation to the opportunities for the particular study of Missouri law and for the observations of local courts, and also in view of the prestige of the Missouri Law School among the citizens of the state, his prospective clients. (*Missouri ex rel Gaines v. Canada*, 305 U.S. 236, 83 L.Ed 213)

The *Gaines* decision was reaffirmed by the Court's ruling in *Sipuel v. Board of Regents* when the University of Oklahoma was ordered to admit Ada Sipuel, an African American student to its law school (*Sipuel v. Board of Regents*, 1948.)

Again, the Supreme Court invalidated segregated colleges because the facilities provided for African-Americans were found to be inferior to those provided for whites. The emphasis once again shifted from "separate" to equal."

The challenge to the doctrine of *separate but equal* continued when H. M. Sweatt, a Texas postal worker challenged the law. In 1946, he applied for admission to the University of Texas Law School. During this era, African Americans were denied admission to all law schools in Texas; therefore, Sweatt's application was rejected. He filed a lawsuit against the university demanding admission to their law school (Rotunda, 1993). The university was aware of the 1938 *Gaines* decision and therefore realized that Sweatt's lawsuit could not be taken lightly. In response to this lawsuit, in 1947, the state established a temporary law school in Austin, Texas especially for African Americans. A permanent law school was established later in Houston (Rotunda, 1993). Sweatt challenged the university's separate but equal doctrine. He contended that the law school established for African Americans was inferior to the law school attended by Whites; however, the Texas courts found that the two schools were equal. Sweatt appealed this decision to the Supreme Court.

Thurgood Marshall, chief counsel for the NAACP, asked the court to repudiate the doctrine of "separate but equal" as applied to the field of education. Marshall contended that this doctrine was unconstitutional and violated the Fourteenth Amendment. The Supreme Court's ruling did not repudiate the doctrine of separate but equal; however, the court declared that Texas had not provided an equal law school as required under this doctrine. The court ruled:

> In terms of the number of faculty, variety of courses and opportunity for specialization, size of the student body, scope of the library, availability of the law review and similar activities, the University of Texas Law School is superior. What is more important, the University of Texas law School possesses to a greater degree those qualities which are incapable of greater measurement but which make for greatness in a law school. Such qualities to name but a few, include reputation of faculty, experience of the administration, position and influence of the alumni, standing in the community, traditions and prestige. (*Sweatt v. Painter*, 1950)

The concept of equality was also examined by the courts in *Sweatt v. Painter* (1950) in which the Supreme Court ruled that the state of Texas could not provide African American students with an equal education in a separate law school. The fact that the facilities at the University of Texas law School were superior to those of the African American law school was not the decisive factor in this ruling. The decisive factor was the fact that the University of Texas "possesses a far higher degree those qualities which are incapable of objective measurement but which make for greatness in a law school. The Supreme Court, in the evaluation of the two law schools, considered additional factors. The court ruled:

> Moreover, although the law is a highly learned profession we are well aware that it is an extremely practical one. The law school, the practicing ground for legal learning and practice…cannot be effective in isolation from the individuals and institutions with which the law interacts. Few students and no one who has practiced law would choose to study in an academic vacuum, removed from the interplay of ideas and the exchange of views with which the law is concerned. The law school of Texas is willing to admit petitioner excludes from its student body members of the racial groups which number 85 percent of the state and include most of the lawyers, witnesses, jurors, judges and other officials with whom he will inevitably be dealing with when he becomes a member of the Texas bar. With such a substantial and significant society excluded, we cannot conclude that the education offered petitioner is substantially equal to that which he would receive if admitted to the University of Texas Law School. (*Sweatt v. Painter* 339, US, 634, 1950)

During the 1950s, the court began to reconsider the doctrine of *separate but equal* as applied to education. In 1950, G. W. McLaurin, an African American graduate student, was ordered admitted to the University of Oklahoma by a federal judge. Because McLaurin was African American, the university developed different rules for him. He was required to sit in specific seats in the classroom and the cafeteria and use the facilities that had been designated "for coloreds only." Additional challenges to the to the "separate but equal" doctrine was presented in the 1950 *McLaurin v. Oklahoma State Board of Regents for Higher Education,* the Supreme Court ruled that African American students should be treated like all others and not segregated within the institution. As was the case in *Sweatt,* the judge ruled that engaging in discussion and exchanging ideas with other students are "intangible considerations, indispensable to equal educational opportunities" (*McLaurin v. Oklahoma State Board of Regents For Higher Education,* 1950). Unlike the *Plessy* decision, the higher-education challenges to the *separate but equal* doctrine emphasized the intangibles that courts must consider in interpreting the equal protection clause of the Fourteenth Amendment.

SEPARATE BUT EQUAL IN PUBLIC EDUCATION: *BROWN V. TOPEKA BOARD OF EDUCATION*

The higher education cases directly impacted the 1954 *Brown* decision, which held that segregated schooling that had been invalidated in *Sweatt* and *McLaurin* was universally harmful to African American students. The NAACP Legal Defense Fund decided to challenge the doctrine of *separate but equal* in the nation's public schools. Thurgood Marshall led the legal battle and argued the case of *Brown v. the Board of Topeka, Kansas.* This decision was a consolidation ruling that included the states of Kansas, Virginia, Delaware, South Carolina, and the District of Columbia. Much like little Sarah Roberts, Linda Brown was an eleven-year-old African American student who attended a segregated school in Topeka, Kansas. Although the nearest school to Linda was only five blocks from her house, she was required to attend a school located miles from her house (Barnes, 1983).

Linda was not allowed to attend the school near her home because it was an all-White school. The school attended by Linda Brown was comparable to the White school in terms of the physical plant, curricula, teacher salaries, and teacher qualifications (Barnes, 1983). These school characteristics reflected the tangible, measurable variables associated with schooling. Unlike the previous higher- education cases—*Sweatt, McLaurin,* and *Gaines*—the courts could not order the all-White school to admit Linda Brown on the basis of that school's superiority. The high court was forced to consider that concept of segregation and its social and academic dynamics was opposed to the doctrine of *separate but equal.* The issue of legally compelled segregation became the focus of *Brown v. Topeka, Kansas Board of Education.* At issue in this case was whether the states had the constitutional power to segregate African American and White students in separate elementary and secondary public schools. These cases were sponsored by the NAACP Legal Committee and argued before the Supreme Court by the NAACP lawyers. These lawyers acted on behalf of Linda's father, Oliver and the parents of twelve additional African American schoolchildren (Barnes, 1983). The legal team contended that segregation is discrimination and therefore, a violation of the Equal Protection Clause of the Fourteenth Amendment.

The lower courts' rulings in these cases were based on the doctrine of *separate but equal,* under which segregation was sustained as long as facilities for African-Americans and whites were equal. The doctrine of *separate but equal,* handed down in the 1896 *Plessy* decision, was viewed by the courts as a mistake. This became evident in 1954 when the Supreme Court found that Topeka, Kansas operated a dual school system with separate facilities for African Americans and Whites. The court ruled:

> We conclude that in the field of public education the doctrine of separate but equal the doctrine of has no place. Separate educational facilities are inherently unequal. (U.S. Commission on Civil Rights, 1975)

Chief Justice Earl Warren delivered the unanimous decision of the court that quoted the passages from *Sweatt* and *McLaurin,* which emphasized the intangible considerations affecting equal educational opportunity settings:

> Such considerations apply with added force to children in grade and high school. To separate them (African-American children) from others of similar age and qualifications solely because of race generates a feeling of inferiority as to their status in the community that may affect their hearts and minds in ways unlikely to be undone. (*Brown v. Topeka, Kansas, Board of Education,* 1954)

The Chief Justice quoted this finding from the lower court in the *Brown* decision. He further stated that:

> Segregation of white and colored children in public schools has a detrimental effect upon the colored children. The impact is greater when it has the sanction of the law; for the policy of separating the races is usually interpreted as denoting the inferiority of the Negro group. A sense of inferiority affects the motivation of a child to learn. Segregation with the sanction of the law, therefore, has a tendency to retard the education and mental development of Negro children and to deprive them of some of the benefits they would receive in a racially integrated school system. (*Brown v. Topeka Kansas, Board of Education,* 1954)

The *Brown* decision resulted in the court ruling that legally compelled segregation of students by race is a deprivation of the Equal Protection law as guaranteed by the Fourteenth Amendment. Although the ruling in *Brown* was directed against legally sanctioned segregation, the language in the Brown decision supported a broader interpretation. The court recognized the inherent inequality of all segregation, noting only that the sanction of the law gives it greater effect. This ruling reflected a concern for segregation resulting from factors other than legally compulsion. De jure, segregation refers to deliberate official segregation of students on the basis of race, as in the school districts represented by the *Brown* decision and other school districts operating under state law requiring separation. De facto segregation refers to racial segregation that results from illegal actions of school officials, for example through gerrymandering or attendance boundaries.

Although the May 17 *Brown* decision declared that segregation in public education was unconstitutional, this ruling was followed by the May 31, 1955 *Brown II* Decision which stated that "all provisions of federal, state or local law requiring or permitting segregation in public education must yield to the principle announced in the 1954 Decision." The 1954 *Brown* decision provided the avenue through which the public schools could begin to desegregate their districts voluntarily. One year after *Brown I*, strategies for the elimination of segregation were argued before the Supreme Court. The court established a standard for the implementation of desegregation. The 1955 *Brown II* decision required a "good faith" start in the transformation from dual to unitary education systems under the jurisdiction of district courts, "with all deliberate speed." (United States Commission on Civil Rights, 1977). The court also permitted limited delays in achieving complete desegregation if a school board could establish that such time is necessary in the public interest (*Brown v. Topeka, Kansas Board of Education*, 1954).

In the area of higher education, the Supreme Court ruled in *Hawkins v. Board of Control of Florida* that "all deliberate speed" was applicable only to elementary and high schools. The immediate right to equal education remained intact at all levels of education beyond secondary school (United States Commission on Civil Rights, 1977).

On April 20, 1971, Chief Justice Burger wrote a decision in which all members of the Supreme Court concurred. This case dealt with busing problems. In *Swann v. Charlotte-Mecklenburg Board of Education*, the Supreme Court sustained a national desegregation plan requiring extensive busing. The court ruled that cities whose schools had historically been segregated by law could not defend continuing school desegregation after they have adopted a neighborhood school plan. The school must be actually integrated no matter how much hardship and extra transportation are involved. The court mandated an acceptable bus transportation plan: grouping of noncontiguous school plans, the elimination of single-race schools, and the utilization of African American and European American ratios in desegregation. The primary concern in *Swann* was the school assignment plan.

THE IMPACT OF *BROWN*

In the 1930s, the NAACP devised a plan to legally dismantle segregation in the nation's public schools. Against the backdrop of the New Deal Era, the attorneys for the NAACP decided that the political climate in the country had become somewhat liberal. The assumption was that the public would support public policies that sought equal access to educational opportunities; however, these same individuals would not support social integration between African American and European Americans. In 1933, Nathan Margold, a European American Harvard law school graduate, published a report that outlined legal strategies for challenging the application of the doctrine of *separate but equal* to public schools. (Wexler, 1993). The lawyers' challenge was based upon the fact that the justices based their decisions handed down in *Plessy v. Ferguson* on case law that predated the Civil War and the Fourteenth Amendment.

During the twenty-five years prior to the *Brown* decision, the Supreme Court ruled in several decisions that the *separate but equal* doctrine violated the Equal Protection Clause of the Fourteenth Amendment (Leflar & Davis, 1954). These cases had a direct influence upon the 1954 *Brown* decision. In *Gaines ex rel Missouri v. Canada* and *Sipuel v. Board of Regents* (1948), the United States Supreme Court invalidated school desegregation because the facilities provided for African Americans were found to be unequal to those provide for European Americans. In 1950, the Supreme Court stipulated that the physical structures and other facets of a school program were not the only considerations in determining educational opportunity. However, the entire educational experience needed to be considered (United States Commission on Civil Rights, 1977).

CHAPTER 4

VIRGINIA'S MASSIVE RESISTANCE TO DESEGREGATION

What Happened in Norfolk?

Desegregation is not just sitting next to someone of another race.
Economic class and family and community educational background
are also critically important for educational opportunity.

—Orfield, Bachmier, James, and Elite (1997)

The city of Norfolk is located in the southeastern region of the state of Virginia and is home to the largest urban school district in the state. The school district employs approximately 33,000 students and employs 5,500 in 62 facilities (Norfolk Public Schools, 2008). Norfolk is located in the southeastern region of Virginia along the Elizabeth River. The city is also home to the world's largest naval base. Its strategic location along the mouth of the Chesapeake Bay makes it a cultural and financial regional power. Norfolk has long been the center of trade, transportation and military operations. According to the 2004 census, 241,727 reside in the city. An elaborate network of highways, bridges and tunnels connect the cities of Norfolk, Virginia Beach, Newport News, Hampton Chesapeake, Portsmouth and Suffolk. These seven independent municipalities are located in the metropolitan

Narrowing the Achievement Gap in a (Re)Segregated Urban School District, pages 41–56
Copyright © 2009 by Information Age Publishing

area known as Hampton Roads. The Hampton Roads region has a population of just over 1.5 million (Norfolk Census Tracts, 2000).

A review of race/ethnic demographics revealed the following divisions: 48.4% European American; 44.1% African American; .05% American Indian; 2.8% Asian American; 0.01% Native American; 1.7% other race; 2.5% biracial or multiracial; 3.8% Latino. The district's most recent profile is listed in Table 4.1. The district's 2008 enrollment is 35,610 students of which 59% receive free or reduced lunch and have been categorized as economically disadvantaged. Approximately 23.7% of the students attending the district's public schools are European American; 63.9%; are African American; 3.9% are Hispanic; 2.4% are Asian/Pacific Islander; and 0.25% are American Indian/Pacific Islander students. The overall proficiency rate on the Standard of Learning tests is 80.6% in reading and 72.5% in mathematics.

Since the early 1950s, the economic stability of the city has been centered on its shipyards, seaport and naval base. Norfolk's quest for equal education for African American students must be discussed within changing dynamics of the 1950s political arena. One cannot discuss specifics of Virginia's massive resistance to school desegregation without addressing the political conservatism enveloping the state during the *Brown* Era. At this time, United States Senator, Harry F. Byrd was the most influential political figure in the state. Senator was the chief supporter and developer of the massive resistance program. He believed that the federal government had no right to interfere with state and local issues. The senator referred to the 1954 *Brown* decision as: "the most serious blow that has been struck against the rights of states" (Muse, 1961, p. 5). Byrd's contention reflected a racist view that African American and European American students should not be mixed; therefore, he strategically developed plans of massive resistance

TABLE 4.1 Norfolk City Public Schools Profile 2008

SOL pass rate	
Reading proficiency	80.6
Mathematics proficiency	72.5
Students per pupil	11.2
Enrollment	35,610
Economically Disadvantaged	
Race/ethnicity	
European American	23.7
African American	63.9
Hispanic	3.9
Asian/Pacific Islander	2.4
Native Indian/Alaska native	0.2

that would keep Virginia's public schools segregated. Massive resistance to school desegregation began in 1954 and ended in 1959.

RESISTING SCHOOL DESEGREGATION

The fight for "state's rights" and segregated schooling began on August 3, 1954, Governor Thomas B. Stanley of Virginia appointed state senator Garland Gray as chair of a 32-member committee charged with investigating the impact of the 1954 *Brown* decision on the state; to propose alternative strategies to federal mandate and make recommendations to the governor (Campbell, 1960). The committee released its findings on November 11, 1955. (See Table 4.2.)

The Gray committee suggested that the governor should require: (a) public school districts that allow European American and African American students to attend school together would not receive any funding to support public education from the state of Virginia, (b) local school boards would be allowed to transfer and utilize funds to award grants to students attending private non-sectarian schools, (c) the placement of students in the public schools and school attendance districts would be determined by a special state board appointed by the governor, and (d) the state of would mandate segregated public schooling and any district attempting to desegregate would be removed from the public school system (Muse, 1961).

TABLE 4.2   Summary of Virginia's Massive Resistance Plan

Chapter	Policy Provision
71	Any elementary or secondary schools enrolling European and African American students together will be stripped of state funds. Additionally funding will be provided only for efficient schools. Efficient schools are defined as racially segregated schools.
56	Funds withheld from schools designated as non-efficient public schools will be made available to nonsectarian private schools to compensate school personnel.
62	Local school boards may transfer and award grants to students who choose to attend private, nonsectarian schools.
70	A Student's Placement Board would make all decisions relevant to student placement, and attendance districts for all public schools in the state of Virginia.
68	The state of Virginia will assume control of any school in which European American and African American students are enrolled by any school authority acting voluntarily or under federal mandate. These schools will be closed and removed from the public school system and control will be given to the governor.

Source: Summarized from Campbell, 1961

The state of Virginia developed and implemented policies designed to avoid the United States Supreme Court's mandate in the 1954 *Brown* decision. The state developed program that was described as "massive resistance." The philosophy of the massive resistance program reflected the philosophy that racial segregation was socially desirable and should be perpetuated. As Campbell, (1960) noted, as soon as one plan of resistance was successfully defeated, another plan was developed and implemented. Philosophically, the advocates of the massive resistance plan contended that the 1954 *Brown* decision violated the United States Constitution and was therefore void (Ely, 1976). It is also interesting to note that President Dwight D. Eisenhower did not voice any opinion about Virginia' Massive Resistance Movement. He was advised by his press secretary, James C. Haggarty that:

> No comment be made which would be interpreted as either as approving resistance or disapproving the vote of Virginia . . . rather, the President might well point out that pursuant to the vote, a state wide plan will be formulated to deal with the issues of segregation in the school. (Ely, 1976)

The parents in the city continued to challenge segregated schooling for their children. They contended that the segregated African American schools were inferior in every way to those attended by European American. Leola Beckett, formed an alliance with other African American parents and the NAACP and sued the Norfolk City School Board for maintaining segregated schools. In *Beckett v. School Board City of Norfolk*, the plaintiffs challenged the state's Student Placement Law, which allowed the state board to reject African applicants.

The 1956 session of the Virginia Assembly signaled the beginning of the Era of Massive Resistance in the state of Virginia. The battle for school desegregation continued for more than a decade. Virginia and other southern states resisted desegregation through a variety of tactics, especially the development of freedom of choice plans. Freedom of choice plans served to perpetuate segregated school districts (Ely, 1976). At this time, Norfolk was considered one of the most liberal cities in south and was not viewed as a primary player in the massive resistance movement. However, the city played an important role in the massive resistance movement. On August 18, 1958, the Norfolk School Board met to consider the applications of 151 African American junior and senior high school students for admission to the public schools within the city. Prior to this time, no African American children were allowed to attend school with European American children. At the August 15, 1958 meeting, the school board rejected the applications of the African American students (Muse 1961). The school board cited the possibility of racial confrontations as the primary rationale for rejecting the applicants. United States District Judge Walter E. Hoffman rejected the validity of the school board's decision and ordered the students admitted. The Norfolk School Board decided to admit 17 of the 151 African American students to six all European American junior and senior high schools. These African American students (the Norfolk 17) were required to take rigorous and psychological tests administered by the Norfolk School Board (Campbell, 1960). The judge's actions presented a conflict between state and federal law in the state of Virginia. The laws of the state of Virginia required the governor of the state to seize control and close any public schools, which were required to admit African Americans. On September 28, 1958, Governor James Almond who succeeded Governor Stanley, closed Norfolk's six European American high schools, which had an aggregate enrollment of 10,000 students. These schools were closed by an act of the Virginia Legislature. As Muse noted:

> The parents now set about frantically to find schools for their children to attend. Some who could afford the expense placed them in private schools. Exiles from Norfolk were scattered over twenty-nine states. In Norfolk, three thousand children were deprived of any schooling at all and four thousand were attending tutorial classes. (pp. 158–162)

James H. Hershman (1998) reported that:

> In the six months from November 1958 to April 1958, Virginia's Massive resistance program to block public desegregation collided with two forces strong enough to cause its demise: The federal courts and a pro-public education citizens' Movement. Backed by the national government's power, federal judges overturned the school closing laws adopted by the General Assembly in 1956 and 1958; but, the federal judiciary was bound by constitutional limitations. It could not, for example, restrain the State government from removing its commitment to public education from the Virginia constitution and promoting the establishment of publicly subsidized segregated public schooling. (p. 104)

On January 19, 1959, three judges from the Federal District Court of Norfolk ruled that "the school closing statutes and the governor's Norfolk school closing order in violation of the 14th amendment to the United States Constitution and therefore void" (Muse, 1960, p. 182).

THE NORFOLK CITY PUBLIC SCHOOL DISTRICT DESEGREGATES

The Supreme Court's decision on May 17, 1954 declared that the practice of segregating students in public school districts unconstitutional; however, a dual education system continued to thrive in Norfolk. On February 2, 1959, the Norfolk 17 African American Students were the first to attend an all European American school in the city. By 1962, little progress had been noted in Norfolk's desegregation efforts. There were 33 all European American and 24 all African American schools in the district (Baker, 1962). It is also interesting to note that there were 10 integrated schools consisting of 12,922 students of which only 101 were African American. No European Americans attended majority African American schools (Baker, 1962). In 1968, the district had 73 public schools with an enrollment of 55,449 students. Ten of these schools were 100% European American and 19 were 100% African American; nine schools were 99% European American or African American. Additional analysis of data revealed that 10 were 97% European American or African American; eleven were over 90% European American of African American. In sum, 59 of the 73 schools were more than 90% European American or African American. This indicated that more than 45,000 of the 55,000 students attended racially segregated schools (Norfolk Public Schools Special Report on Enrollment, 1968). By 1970, The city's of resistance to school desegregation had grown and the litigate continued when in 1970 African American parents once again filed suit in *Brewer v. School Board the City of Norfolk*. At this time, there were 55 elementary schools in the city and 86% of all African American students were enrolled in 22 of these schools, which were more than 92% African American. On the other hand, 81% of the European American children attended 25 schools that were more than 92% European American. Eight schools had African American enrollments from 10% to 75%. (*Brewer v. School Board City of Norfolk*, 1970). During the 1969–1970 school year, 56,600 students were enrolled in the district. Of this total, 32,600 were European American and 24, 000, were African American. One of the districts five high schools was 100% African American and it enrolled more than 50% of the city's senior high school students. A review of statistics indicated that the remaining four schools had enrollment levels ranging from 9% to 53% African American (*Brewer v. School Board of City of Norfolk*, 1970).

The United States District Court for the Eastern District of Virginia ruled that Norfolk must develop a school plan that would eliminate racially identifiable schools in its district. As a result of this decision, the Norfolk school District was required to desegregate. The court placed the primary responsibility for eliminating segregated schools on the local boards of education. The public schools in Norfolk did not desegregate until January 1970. The school district utilized clustering and pairing techniques as methods of desegregation. Busing was instituted to facilitate the integration of the public schools. Under the leadership of school superintendent Dr. Albert Ayars, the mandate issued by the Supreme Court in *Green v. New Kent County School*

Board was implemented. In the *Green* decision, the court ordered school districts to take whatever steps necessary to convert from a dual educational system to a unitary system. In *Green*, the court stated that the primary indication of a segregated school system was racial discrimination in faculty, staff, transportation, extra curricula activities and facilities. The ruling further cited that as long as a school remains racially identifiable, in terms of the racial composition of the staff and teachers, segregation still exists.

As indicated in Table. 4.3, the percentage of European American students attending public schools in the city of Norfolk declined from 60% during the 1967–1968 academic year to 41% in 1982. The total enrolment also declined from 56,384 students to 35,320 during this same period of time. In 1971, a federal judge approved a desegregation plan that required cross-town busing between paired schools. Almost 50% of the students were transported to new schools.

Busing eliminated the all-African-American schools; however, the percentage of African American students in some of the schools was between 65% and 70%. The Norfolk School District adopted and implemented a student assignment plan similar to that approved by the Supreme Court in *Swann v.*

TABLE 4.3   Norfolk City Schools Percentage European American 1967–1982

	White	Black	Total	Percentage White[a]
1967–68	33,838	22,546	56,384	60.00
1968–69	33,103	23,023	56,126	59.00
1969–70	32,586	24,244	56,830	57.00
1970–71	30,246	24,425	54,671	55.32
1971–72	25,858	23,930	49,788	51.94
1972–73	24,224	23,578	47,802	50.68
1973–74	24,337	24,714	49,051	49.62
1974–75	23,536	24,451	47,987	49.05
1975–76	22,957	24,420	47,377	48.46
1976–77	22,080	23,976	46,056	47.94
1977–78	20,412	23,282	43,694	46.72
1978–79	18,913	22,686	41,599	45.47
1979–80	16,373	21,395	37,768	43.35
1980–81	15,629	21,014	36,643	42.65
1981–82	14,435	20,885	35,320	40.87

[a] White includes approximately 3% other minority races
Source: Riddick v. School Bd., No. 84-1815, United States Court of Appeals for the Fourth Circuit, 784 F.2d 521; 1986 U.S. App.

Charlotte-Mecklenburg Board of Education. The *Swann* decision approved mandated busing of children to remedy past constitutional breaches. Judge Burger issued the unanimous decision and stated:

> All things being equal, with no history of discrimination, it might well be desirable to assign pupils to schools nearest their homes. But not all things are equal in a system that has been deliberately constructed and maintained to enforce racial desegregation. The remedy for such segregation may be administratively awkward, inconvenient and even bizarre in some situations and may impose burdens on some. (*Swann v. Charlotte-Mecklenburg Board of Education*)

This case established guidelines for desegregating public schools and gave states oversight of local compliance. The federal court ordered school districts to develop and partially implement a desegregation plan in 1970 and to fully put it into full effect in 1971. A summary of the mandate is displayed in Table 4.4. The Norfolk district implemented mandates set forth in both

TABLE 4.4   Norfolk City Schools Desegregation Plan 1970–1985

Mandate	Implementation
Faculty desegregation	Each school should closely reflect the existing race distribution at the elementary middles and elementary school levels
Free transportation	Prior to 1971, school transportation was furnished by private municipal transit organizations which were not under the supervision of the Norfolk School Board
	A fare was charged to the students by the transit company and the. The court ruled that this charge placed an unfair burden on the plaintiffs and therefore the court ordered the school board to provided free transportation. The court further ruled that it would not approve any desegregation plan that placed an unfair burden on African American children.
Student assignment	The school board was ordered to devise a plan that would eliminate the racial identity of each elementary school and to file this plan with the court for review and approval.
Majority–minority transfer	The court stated that the desegregation plan must provide students with the option of transferring to schools where their race was in the minority.
Regulations	School attendance boundaries will not be drawn to assign students to racially identifiable (fewer than 30 or more than 70% minority or majority students) schools.
	Attendance patterns must be devised that will allow students to be assigned to schools near their neighborhoods for part of the elementary grades. Single attendance zones should be created when possible.

the *Swann* and *Green* rulings. Under the Norfolk plan (Table 4.4) students were assigned so that each school reflected the racial composition of the total system. More than 24,000 students were bused to achieve mandated desegregated (Jewell-Jackson, 1996). It was the Supreme Court decision in *Swann* that added fuel to the city's desegregation efforts. Finally, on February 1975, the United States District Court for Eastern Virginia acknowledged Norfolk's achievement and declared it to be a unitary school system:

> It appears to the court that all issues in this action have been disposed of, that the school Board of the city of Norfolk has certified its affirmative duty to desegregate, that racial discrimination through official action has been eliminated from the system and that the Norfolk School System is now unitary.

RETHINKING NEIGHBORHOOD SCHOOLS

Between 1960 and 1980, the European American population in the city of Norfolk declined by 28%, while the African American population increased by 19%. Many European Americans began to move to the suburbs of Virginia Beach and Chesapeake. By 1980, the African American population was 35% and European American enrollment in public schools was 60%. Shifting demographics led the Norfolk School Board to propose a plan that would return students to neighborhood schools (Carr & Zeigler, 1990). The Norfolk School Board met during the 1981–82 school year and formed a committee to consider a reduction in cross-town busing for integration. The committee visited Shreveport, Louisiana and consulted with scholars David Armor, Ron Edmonds, Sarah Lightfoot, and Robert Green. Dr. David Armor's report indicated that white flight in the district was a problem. He also contended that:

> Mandatory busing had led to significant white flight and that if busing continued, the Norfolk school system would be 75% black by 1987. At the point of 75% black, no matter in which year it occurred, of course the average black child could not expect to be educated in a desegregated school according to the 70/30 definition used and which Armor stated was consistent with most definitions of segregation. Busing, he said, had aided the obtainment of racial balance but such balance was of little aid as the system was resegregating with the rapid loss of white students. He concluded that under such circumstances, busing did not significantly aid black academic achievement and that white student enrollment would stabilize if busing were eliminated (Civil Rights Monitor, 1986).

The Board proposed a return to neighborhood schools and that the city abolishes the policy of mandated cross-town busing for segregation. This proposed policy shift resulted in heated debates throughout the city. Some African American parents believed that busing had resulted in equalizing opportunities for their children. They believed that academic performance would increase for their children and that the African American/European American achievement gap would decrease. One is reminded of John Rawl's principles of justice that contend: (1) "each person is to have an equal right to the most extensive scheme of equal basic liberties compatible with a similar scheme of liberties for others" and (2) "they are to be of the greatest benefit to the least-advantaged members of society; offices and positions must be open to everyone under conditions of fair equality of opportunity" (Rawls, 1999), p. 303). Rawl's principles suggest that busing as a remedy for past constitutional violations would not result in equal social and economic opportunities for African American children.

It can be argued that access to education and social equality are not linear. Many individuals in the city of Norfolk sought to strike a balance between mandated busing and freedom of choice. Busing eliminated neighborhood schools an educational option.

Those parents who enjoyed higher socioeconomic status had choices that their lower status counterparts did not posses. Those parents with greater financial resources were able to divorce themselves from the policy of mandated busing by enrolling their children in private schools. This often was not available to many parents with limited resources. Mandated busing policies also encouraged many middle class African American and European American parents to explore other options for their children. These parents often moved from their communities in order to avoid mandated busing. As a result of parents exercising their freedom of choice rights, property values often declined, causing a reduction in property taxes. Parents who opposed the return to neighborhood schools in the city of Norfolk contended that as a result of elimination of busing for desegregation, at least 10 to 12 schools would become 100 African American (Table 4.5.) They also noted that the city was becoming resegregated; therefore, equality in the allocation of resources would not be realized for African American children.

It can be argued that access to education and social equality are not linear. Many individuals in the city of Norfolk sought to strike a balance between mandated busing and freedom of choice. Busing eliminated neighborhood schools as an educational option. Therefore, equality in the allocation of resources would not be realized for African American children. After reviewing their reports, a series of meetings was held with citizens throughout the city to discuss proposed plans. The primary issue concerned the status of African-American children in the city of Norfolk who were assigned to all African-American schools. Many parents contended that African-American children would suffer educationally and socially in these segregated schools. The school board members sought to eliminate such fears by pro-

TABLE. 4.5 Norfolk City Schools Projected Elementary School Enrollment after School Resegregation in Norfolk–1986

School	Projected elementary enrollment		
	Assignment	White %	Black%
Bay View	710	84	16
Bowling Park	589	1	99
Calcott	563	61	39
Camp Allen	689	62	38
Chesterfield	572	1	99
Coleman Place	970	47	53
Crossroads	714	37	63
Diggs Park	381	2	98
Fairlawn	282	73	27
Granby Elementary	674	44	56
Ingleside	665	38	62
Jacox	769	1	99
Larchmont	685	52	48
Larrymore	768	31	69
Lindenwood	492	21	79
Little Creek Elementary & Primary	1037	75	25
Meadowbrook	512	61	39
Monroe	831	0	100
Norview	602	32	68
Oakwood	415	35	65
Oceanair	672	71	29
Oceanview	586	78	22
Poplar Halls	388	43	57
Roberts Park	401	0	100
St. Helena	355	2	98
Sewells Point	664	64	36
Sherwood Forrest	627	70	30
Suburban Park	539	55	45
Tarrallton	548	48	52
Taylor	487	54	46
Tidewater Park	276	2	98
Tucker	312	3	97
Willard	802	26	74
Willoughby	558	65	35
Young Park	510	1	99
Ghent	600	(open classroom program)	

Source: Riddick v. School Bd., No. 84-1815, United States Court of Appeals for the Fourth Circuit, 784 F.2d 521; 1986 U.S. App.

posing: an expansion of pre-kindergarten programs to include four year
olds from lower income homes; a program to increase parental involvement in schools attended primarily by African-American children; a school
effectiveness program to ensure that poor children would learn at the same
rate as the more affluent students.

The proposal to eliminate mandated busing for desegregation and to return to neighborhood schools met with much opposition from the community. The Representative Council of the Education Association of Norfolk
issued the following statement:

> The Education Association of Norfolk opposes any effort to reduce busing
> that would cause any schools to resegregate. The school board is urged to
> strongly consider routes that will reduce travel time but will maintain racial
> balance with a minimum amount of disruption in terms of student/teacher
> reassignments. Additionally, we reaffirm our opposition to the magnet school
> concept that would create an educational climate which is segregated in terms
> of intellectual, social, cultural, and/or economic status and thus is artificial in
> terms of preparation for life. (Educational Association of Norfolk, 1983)

By 1983, approximately 58% of the students enrolled during this academic year were European American and 42% were African American.

However, this represented a 59% decline in the city's African public school
students from 1960 to 1983 (*Riddick v. School Board City of Norfolk*, 1984). After
the series of public hearings ended, the school board chair, voiced the following: the drawbacks of mandated busing, the rationale, busing as a means of
Equalizing school resources, the relationship between busing and academic
achievement; and busing as a means to end desegregation.

Between 1971 and 1983, the student population decreased by 37%
(21,290), with white students accounting for 90% of the decline (19,259).
School desegregation accounted for the loss of between 6000 and 8000 white
students, and for the last five years the student population has held steady
at approximately 35,000. By 1981, there were seven elementary schools over
70 percent black, and in 1983, the school board voted to end the busing
of elementary school children for school desegregation purposes. (Civil
Rights Monitor, 1986, p. 2)

However, after more than 15 years of mandated busing for integration,
enrollment declines continued and as a result of a loss of more than 18,000
students, the Norfolk School Board suggested a new approach to desegregation. The school board voted 5–2 to abolish cross-town busing for elementary school children. The revised desegregation plan assigned students
to neighborhood schools, creating ten elementary schools that were more
than 95% African American. This new neighborhood schools plan was challenged in the United States District Court for Eastern Virginia. On May 6,
1983, Paul Riddick, Jr. and 21 other African American plaintiffs filed a suit

on behalf all the African American elementary students in the city of Norfolk. The Norfolk School Board was named as defendant in the suit.

The Plaintiffs charged that the school board intentionally adopted an elementary school assignment plan that was unconstitutional and that discriminated against the African American students because of their race. The plaintiffs demanded that the court declare the Norfolk Public Schools student assignment adopted on February 2, 1983, in violation of the 14th Amendment and therefore unconstitutional.

In 1984, Virginia District Court judge, John Mackenzie ruled that the Norfolk Public Schools could end court mandated cross-town busing of elementary students for the purpose of desegregation. The court held that the neighborhood school plan adopted by the Norfolk School Board on February 2, 1983 did not discriminate against African American students because of their race. Additionally, the court ruled that the plaintiffs had failed to show that the school board's assignment plan was motivated by race. The judge stated that there was evidence to show that the district was attempting to address the issues surrounding white flight and to increase parental involvement in the schools. The judge further stated that ending busing for desegregation may have a negative effect on African American students; however, the plaintiffs did not prove that there an intent to discriminate. Therefore, there was no violation (*Riddick v. Norfolk School Board*, 1984).

Riddick and plaintiffs appealed the decision in the Fourth Circuit Court of Appeals. The case was argued in 1985 and in 1986, circuit court Judge Hiram Widener, Jr. upheld the ruling of the district court. As the judge noted:

> The superintendent of schools, Dr. Gene Carter is African American, two of the three regional assistant superintendents are African Americans. The faculty is likewise fully integrated 56%. White and 44% Black. There are 88 principals in the system, 59% are 41% are Black. Given the staff is completely integrated and given that very qualified Blacks are at the top of the organization. The fear that white students will stand to reap some benefit over Black students is totally lacking in credence. (*Riddick v. Norfolk School Board*, 1986)

The Fourth Circuit Court of Appeals rationale for the decision was that although the court originally ordered the district to utilize busing as a means of desegregating the public schools, it withdrew from the case in 1975. In 1975, the court ruled that the Norfolk Public Schools system was unitary. However, the plaintiffs contended that the system had become more segregated since 1975. The court did not agree and issued the following statement:

> Once a constitutional violation has been remedied, any further judicial action regarding student assignments without a new showing of discriminatory

intent would amount to the setting of racial quotas, which have been consistently condemned by the Court in the context of school integration absent a need to remedy an unlawful condition. Racial quotas are to be used as a starting point in remedying de jure segregation but not as an ultimate goal to be continued in perpetuity. . . . We agree with the district court that the evidence reveals that Norfolk's neighborhood school assignment plan is a reasonable attempt by the school board to keep as many white students in public education as possible and so achieve a stably integrated school system. . . . While the effect of the plan in creating several black schools is disquieting, that fact alone is not sufficient to prove discriminatory intent. (*Riddick v. Norfolk School Board*, 1986)

The court further stated:

Our holding is a limited one, applicable only to those school systems, which have succeeded in eradicating all vestiges of de jure segregation. In those systems, the school boards and not the federal courts will run the schools, absent a showing of intent to discriminate. We do not think this is a case in which a school board, upon obtaining a judicial decision that it is unitary, turns its back on the rights of its minority students and reverts to its old discriminating ways. If such were the case, we would, of course, not approve Norfolk's new assignment plan. But such is not the case. The school board of Norfolk has done a reasonable job in seeking to keep its schools integrated in the face of a massive exodus of white students. We should not tie its hands and refuse to allow it to try another plan that may be successful in stopping that exodus. (*Riddick v. Norfolk School Board*, 1986)

THE NORFOLK SCHOOL DISTRICT RESEGREGATES

In 1986, the plaintiffs attempted to get the Supreme Court to review the circuit court's findings; however, the court refused to hear the case. The ruling of the Fourth Circuit Court of Appeals was left intact without approval or disapproval by the United States Supreme Court. Riddick and plaintiffs claimed that the Fourth circuit's ruling reflected beliefs that the findings from the Armor Report (Armor, 1981) was valid and that the city of Norfolk would continue to experience white flight to the suburbs if busing did not end. Additionally the court stated that if busing continued, the Norfolk school district would become majority African American. To support its contention, the court cited a loss of more than 68,000 students as a direct result of busing (Doyle, 2005).

On February 6, 1986, the 4th U.S. Circuit Court of Appeals, finding that 15 years after implementing a court ordered school desegregation plan the system had eliminated all vestiges of segregation, upheld a district court ruling allowing the city of Norfolk to end the busing elementary school children for desegregation purposes. The ruling allows the school board to implement its neighborhood school plan for 35 elementary schools, 10 of which will become virtually all black. The Appeals Court stated, "our holding is a limited one, applicable only to those school systems which have succeeded in eradicating all vestiges of de jure segregation. In those systems the school boards and not the federal courts will run the schools, absent a showing of intent to discriminate." (Civil Rights Monitor, 1986)

The school board projected enrollment was on target. After busing ended, ten elementary schools became 98 to 100 percent African American (Table 4.5). These schools were located in the city's low socioeconomic neighborhood. This return to neighborhood schools also signaled a return to social and economic gaps. The Norfolk Public Schools District ended busing at the elementary level in 1986 and for all middle schools in 2001. It is apparent that since the elimination of busing for desegregation, the district has become resegregated. As Charles Bryant, former President of the Norfolk NAACP stated, in an article written by Mary Doyle: Though segregation diminished and educational opportunities for African Americans improved in the 1970s, in the 1980s, little significant progress was made and the situation began to deteriorate. (Doyle, 2005, pp. 1–17)

Almost five decades after the 1954 *Brown* decision, the doctrine of "separate but equal" continues to be the law of the land in public education. As policymakers at the state and federal levels develop education policies that embrace "separate but equal" in our K–12 public schools, racial isolation increases. Since the 1971 Supreme Court decision in *Swann v. Charlotte-Mecklenburg Board of Education*, the segregation of minority students has increased significantly (Orfield & Eaton, 1996.) Approximately one third of all African American students attend schools where the enrollment is between 90 and 100% minority. Additionally there are more African American children in segregated schools today than in 1954 (Raffel, 1998). In 2001, the Norfolk City Public School District ended cross-town busing for middle school students and 2003 proposed ending busing at the high school level.

Historically, research indicated that the achievement gap between European American children and minority children narrowed significantly from the 1960s to the mid-1990s. The findings further suggest that children attending racially integrated schools perform better than their segregated counterparts (Heubert, 1999.) As McPartland (1968) noted more than three decades ago, racial isolation only serves to increase the achievement gap between African American and European American students. Since the days of the Reagan Administration, the United States Justice Department has done little to force states to comply with desegregation mandates. Affirmative Action programs and other policies designed to assist minority group members in gaining equal access to educational opportunities continue to be challenged by school districts throughout the nation. Attorney General, Reynolds stated, the Norfolk case represented:

> An outline of procedures a school system must follow to free it from court desegregation decrees." While Mr. Reynolds stated that the Department of Justice would not seek "to launch a campaign against busing," he indicated that the Department would have discussions with school districts declared unitary by the courts, and that such districts probably have no reason to delay efforts to end court ordered desegregation plans. According to statistics released by the DOJ, of the 530 school desegregation cases Justice is involved in, 164 have been declared unitary (primarily in Georgia and Alabama). William L. Taylor, director of the Center for National Policy Review and counsel in numerous school desegregation cases, indicated that the decision told school districts, for the first time, that they could institute plans whose effect would be resegregation. (Civil Rights Monitor, 1986)

CHAPTER 5

ACHIEVEMENT GAP RESEARCH

1950s–2008

Two facts about the gap are clear: its origins lie neither in students nor in schools. Skin color, ethnic status, poverty—none of these, by themselves, determine a student's performance.

—Robert Evans, 2004

Chapters 1 and 2 presented discussions of the current state of the achievement gap between African American and European American students. This chapter will review earlier research surrounding the achievement gap between the two groups. *The Nation's Report Card* is a document that tracks and summarizes data from the National Assessment of Educational Progress (NAEP) and publishes NAEP findings relevant to the performance of K–12 students. The report presents analyses of academic progress in reading, writing, science, U.S. history, civics, geography, and other content areas. Analysis of data from the National Assessment of Educational Progress (2007) indicated that the performance of United States students in grade four has improved significantly since 1994. As members of a global society, it is important for all students to have a sense of world history and world cultures. A review of National Assessment of Educational Progress data (2007) suggested that 66% of students in grade four understood the significance of the Statue of Liberty; 35% could elaborate specifics relevant

Narrowing the Achievement Gap in a (Re)Segregated Urban School District, pages 57–77

to how inventions changed lives, and 24% could explain the importance of the western frontier.

Findings also indicated that eighth-grade students showed improvement: 64% were able to discuss the economic and historical importance of the cotton gin; 43.5% knew the goals proposed by Dr. Martin Luther King; whereas only 1% could discuss the historical significance of the Berlin wall. Additionally, European American, African American and Asians showed gains in this area, while their Native American counterparts did not show growth. The four core themes assessed by the NAEP were: (a) Democracy—change and continuity, democracy, and institutions; (b) Culture—gathering and interactions of peoples, cultures and ideas; (c) Technology—economics and technological change, and their relationship to society; (d) world role—the changing role of America in the world (The Nation's Report Card, 2007).

Between 1970 to 1980, the achievement gap between African Americans and European American students declined by 50%. However, the gaps began to widen in 1988 (Haycock, 2001, Forgione, 1998). Analyses of data from the National Center for Educational Statistics (2006) indicated that the standardized achievement test scores of African American students increased significantly in the 1970s, 1980s and 1990s. The results suggested that the reading achievement test scores of 17-year-old African Americans increased throughout the 1980s and 1990; however, the academic gap between African Americans and European Americans increased in the 1990s.

Findings further indicated that the mathematics achievement test scores of 13-year-old African Americans and European American decreased significantly in the 1980s.

A review of findings from the National Center for Educational Statistics (2007) indicated that only 1 in 100 African American 17-year-olds could read and interpret technical data as compared with 1 in 12 of their European American counterparts. Analyses of these data also found that only 1 in 100 African Americans could solve multi-step word problems and elementary algebra as compared to 1 in 10 European American students. Additionally, only 3 in 10 African Americans had mastered the computation of fractions, common percents, and averages, while 7 in 10 European Americans have mastered these skills. The gaps between these two groups continue to pervade the data. The results show that by the end of high school, African Americans had acquired skills in reading and mathematics that are the same as those of eighth-grade European American students. Perhaps even more revealing, the statistics indicated that African Americans are half as likely to complete a four-year college as European Americans.

Although SAT averages increased between 1991 and 2001, there is still a significant gap between African American and European American students (Boehner, 2001). Analyses of data from the National Assessment of

Educational Progress (2000) indicated that the achievement gap between African American and European American students begins in elementary school and continues throughout high school. Between 1971 and 1988, the mathematics achievement gap between African American and European American students declined for 13-year-olds and 17-year-olds. However, From 1988–1996, the gap increased for 13-year-olds and remained constant for 17-year-olds (The Condition of Education, 2000). Further analysis of these data indicated that the average reading score of African American 17-year-olds was 239, which was 22 points below 13-year-old European Americans. In 1988, the average reading score of African American students was 274 and 295 for their European American counterparts. African Americans scored lower than their European American counterparts on vocabulary, reading, and mathematics tests and this deficit continues throughout K–12. African Americans as a group score below 75% of European Americans on most standardized measures (Monk, 2001). The achievement gap between European Americans and African Americans becomes evident in grades, test scores, course selection, and graduation rates (Comer, 2001). By the time African American students complete the fourth grade, these individuals are two years behind their European American counterparts in reading and mathematics achievement. When these African American students begin grade eight, they are at least three years behind; and by grade twelve, they are four years behind (Comer, 2001). The gap between African Americans and Europeans continues to grow throughout the schooling process.

SEGREGATED SCHOOLS AND THE ACHIEVEMENT GAP

A review of previous research relevant to the academic achievement test scores of public school students indicated that, prior to the desegregation of public schools, many districts began to publish results of achievement tests. The results of many of these tests revealed that African American students performed significantly below their European American counterparts. For example, in 1950, a survey conducted in the Dade County, Florida public schools indicated' that eighth-grade European American students performed above the national norm on mathematics achievement test; however, their African American counterparts performed two years below the norm (Weinberg, 1971). Further indications of the race/ethnic academic gap between European American and African American students was re- ported in a survey of public school students conducted in 1954 by the Association of School Administrators (Weinberg, 1971). The results of this study suggested that standardized achievement test scores of European American students were satisfactory while their African American counterparts performed unsatisfactorily on basic content measures. Similar findings were evident in a survey conducted by Ferguson and Plaut (1954) in which thirty-two public schools in eleven states were sampled. This sample was comprised of 10,388 high school seniors, of which, one third was African American. The results indicated that only twenty-four African American students were in the upper quarter of their class. Again the gap was examined in the 1950s when, in a study comparing academic achievement in segregated and desegregated schools, Samuels (1958) found that in grades one and two, African American students in segregated schools performed better than their desegregated counterparts. Additionally, the researcher noted that students in desegregated schools fell further behind European American students during the first grade and that the academic gap stabilized and began to narrow in the second year of schooling. However, he also noted that in grades three, four, and five African American students in desegregated schools performed significantly better than those in the segregated schools. Fortenberry (1959) also found integrated schools to be academically advantageous for African American children. He analyzed the achievement test scores of African American students in the Oklahoma Public Schools District. The scores of eighth and ninth grade African American students were compared with their sixth grade scores. Some of these students had never attended a desegregated school and others had attended segregated schools for seventh and eighth grades. All of these students had statistically similar achievement test scores in grade six. Fortenberry noted that by the time students enter the eighth grade, those attending integrated classes had shown more significant growth in their performance in mathematics when compared to their counterparts attending segregated schools. However, the researcher noted that there was no significant difference in reading achievement test scores. Additional findings from this study indicated that by the time these students entered the ninth grade, students in integrated classes scored higher mathematics and language expression on tests.

Earlier research on the relationship between the achievement gap indicated that in general, African American students perform better in integrated settings. This was evident in the 1960s in a study conducted by Anderson (1966) in which test scores of seventy-five African American fourth-, fifth-, and sixth-grade students in Nashville, Tennessee were compared to a matched sample attending three all African American schools. The students attending the five desegregated schools comprised from 8 to 33% of the total enrollment in their schools and attended desegregated schools for up to six years. All the students in the sample came from the same neighborhood. The results of the study suggested that academic achievement for students attending desegregated schools was much higher than those attending segregated schools. The children attending desegregated schools at the beginning of their education performed significantly better on achievement tests than those attending segregated schools. Additionally, those who were not desegregated until the fifth or sixth grade performed significantly lower on measures of achievement than children in segregated schools.

The early body of scholarly research supports the contention that desegregated settings seem to have a positive effect on the academic achievement of students. Frary and Goolsby (1970) conducted a survey of the academic performance of 450 first graders in Gulfport, Mississippi during the 1968–69 academic year and found that those students with low readiness skills performed at significantly higher levels in integrated first-grade classes than in their previously segregated classes. However, when readiness is held constant, there is no statistically significant difference in performance. Support for these conclusions can be found in a 1978 study conducted by Mahard and Crain (1978) in which they elaborated and published findings on the achievement gap. The researchers studied achievement test performance on each subset of the achievement battery administered in ninety-three studies. They found that desegregation increased each subset equally. Findings also indicated that African American students who showed the smallest growth in test scores in achievement after desegregation had scores in reading comprehension that lagged behind their scores in mathematics, spelling, or vocabulary. The study also concluded that in the school systems where students experienced above-average gains, the reading scores were higher than other subsets of the test. The results of this study suggest that African American students frequently enter desegregated schools with poor reading comprehension skills and are at an academic disadvantage from the beginning of their schooling experience. Mahard and Crain (1978) also concluded that desegregation has a positive effect on African American children's academic achievement. Additionally, they concluded that desegregation may result in better curricula or facilities for African American children. Desegregation may also result in African Americans having better trained or more highly trained teachers. They concluded that the benefits of desegregation do more than improve the academic performance of African American students; it can lead to socioeconomic desegregation. Mahard and Crain (1978) contended that when all of these changes are in place, as a result of desegregation, there will be immediate achievement gains for African American students half or two-thirds of the time.

In an effort to determine the short and long-term effects of desegregation on the academic achievement of African American and European American students. Gerald and Miller (1975) conducted a longitudinal study of the Riverside, California public schools. In the 1965–66 school year, a desegregation plan was implemented in which African Americans and Mexican Americans were bused from low socioeconomic, racially segregated neighborhoods to previously all-European-American schools. The initial sample consisted of 1,731 public school children in grades kindergarten through sixth grade. Standardized achievement test scores, classroom grades, and intellectual ability were used as measures of academic achievement. The results showed that desegregation did not significantly affect the academic performance of minority children and that the test scores of majority students did not decline as a result of desegregation. These questionable findings suggested that desegregation as a variable does not improve the academic achievement of minority students or negatively affect the achievement of European American students. Additionally, results from the National Assessment of Educational Progress, indicated that the mathematic and reading achievement gaps between African American and European American students declined between the 1970s and 2004 (National Assessment of Educational Progress, 2007). Data also indicated that during this period, European American students continued to perform better than their African American and Latino American counterparts. Additional analysis of the NAEP data (Burton and Jones, 1982) found that the average differences in achievement between African Americans and European Americans declined steadily between 1972 and 1982. During the 1970s, researchers focused on a large number of studies that examined student performance in a single community undergoing desegregation and concluded that achievement test scores of European American students are not significantly affected by desegregation. However, these researchers disagreed about the impact of desegregation on the achievement test scores of African American students. Weinberg (1977) reanalyzed many of the same studies and concluded that desegregation increases test scores of African American students. Additional earlier studies have concluded that desegregation is academically beneficial to African American children. For example, Krol (1979) conducted a meta-analysis of a significant number of desegregation studies and concluded that there was a positive relationship between academic achievement and attendance of desegregated schools for African American students.

Research relevant to the effects of desegregation on academic achievement has focused primarily upon African American children. This focus is justifiable given the educational status of African Americans in society. However, there are reasons to consider the outcomes of desegregation for European American children as well. From a policy reform perspective, it is desirable to know if and how integrated classes have affected the academic achievement of European American children. The data from most desegregation studies have failed to consider the costs of desegregation relative its benefits for European American students. In a limited number of studies investigating the achievement of European American students in desegregated settings, results have been mixed. In a few instances, European Americans who usually attend majority African American schools did as well or better than those who attended majority European American schools (St. John, 1975). However, two other studies found a relationship between academic attendance at majority African American schools and lower achievement test scores for European American students (St. John & Lewis, 1971; Wrightstone et al., 1966). On the other hand, studies conducted by Rankin (1972) suggested that there were no negative academic effects for European American students.

Although, St. John and Lewis (1971) found that European American students in predominantly African American schools performed academically below European American students in predominantly European American schools; however, Weinberg (1968) concluded that there was sufficient evidence to suggest that minority group students in integrated settings perform satisfactorily, and that African American students improve academically over an extended period of time. These findings suggested that the achievement gap between the two groups would decline over time.

Several indicators have suggested that the achievement gap between African Americans and European American students was decreasing during the 1980s (Burton & Jones, 1982). Findings indicated that during the 1970s, the discrepancy in average achievement level between African Americans and European Americans was reduced. Burton and Jones noted that, when the achievement of European Americans declined, that of African American students declined less; when European Americans increased, African Americans increased more. The differences between the races decreased in mathematics, science, reading, writing, and social studies. As noted by Weinberg (1983), the body of research related to desegregation tends to support his contention that only a limited number of studies suggested that placing African American students in desegregated schools negatively affect their achievement. Additionally, the literature indicates that there is little evidence to support the contention that desegregation negatively impacts the achievement of European American students.

DESEGREGATED SCHOOLS, RACIAL COMPOSITION AND THE ACHIEVEMENT GAP

The Coleman Report (1966) resulted from a study initiated by the United States Office of Education. The mandate was to conduct a study relevant to the lack of availability of equal educational opportunities for individuals by reason of race, color, religion, or national origin in public institutions. The expected outcomes of this study were that findings would show that school facilities for African American were unequal in comparison to those for European Americans and that the inequality found in these facilities was the direct cause of the achievement gap between African Americans and

European Americans. However, the Coleman Report did not reflect the expected outcomes. The reported stated:

> Differences in school facilities and curriculum, which are the major variables by which attempts are made to improve schools, are so little related to differences in achievement levels of students, that with few exceptions, their effects fail to appear even in a survey of this magnitude. (Coleman, 1966, p. 316)

The Coleman Report (1966) also indicated that the achievement gap between European American and African American students continued to increase throughout subsequent school years. The report also found that the proportion of European American students in a school was positively related to verbal achievement, but these findings disappeared when student characteristics were controlled. A reanalysis of the Coleman data (Cohen, Pettigrew, & Riley, 1972) supported Coleman's findings that the racial composition of the school had little effect upon the verbal achievement of African Americans when school quality and background of individuals are controlled. However, McPartland (1968) reported that school desegregation is associated with higher achievement for African American students only if they attend predominantly European American classrooms and that classroom desegregation is desirable and beneficial regardless of European American students in schools.

The Coleman Report had a profound impact on education policy and issues surrounding the education of African American children. In 1967, the Civil Rights Commission conducted a study on the degree of racial isolation in the public schools. The findings supported the Coleman Report. As a direct result of these two reports, the federal government implemented affirmative action programs and other initiatives to address de facto desegregation. The desegregation policies sought to eliminate racial isolation in the public schools by preventing the percentage of African Americans enrolled in individual schools from exceeding 60 percent.

These changes signaled a policy shift, and school districts throughout the country were forced to develop and implement desegregation plans. Cohen (1967) attempted to examine the effect of racial composition on the academic achievement of white students. He used data from the Civil Rights Commission Report. Cohen noted that there were substantial changes in European American performance associated with changes in racial composition of schools and classrooms. This study also indicated that these differences in performance appeared to operate independently of the students' socioeconomic level. Therefore, whether or not European American's parents were well educated or poorly educated, those in 50% African American classes performed at lower levels than those in more than 50% European American classes. According to Cohen, "when students of any social class level are in majority advantaged schools, there is no apparent negative effect of a majority African American student body " (p. 287). As a result of this study, Cohen concluded that racial composition appears to effect the achievement of European American students. He noted that the same schools that are majority disadvantaged which have low-achieving African American students, also produce low achievement for European American students. Other studies also suggest that there is a strong a relationship between academic achievement and school racial composition. One such study was conducted by Lesser (1964). This was a five-year study in New York City that included 400 children—African American, Puerto Rican, Chinese, and Jewish. Children in more integrated schools and neighborhoods scored higher on achievement measures in verbal ability, reasoning, numerical ability, and space conceptualization. He contended that children attending racially balanced schools showed similar levels of achievement and, when children attend racially imbalanced schools, they perform significantly lower on achievement tests than children who attend racially balanced schools.

It was in the mid-1960s when Matzen (1965) conducted a study, in the San Francisco Bay area, on the effects of racial composition upon academic achievement. Eleven hundred students in eleven schools were tested; only African Americans and European Americans were included in the sample. Findings indicated that, academic achievement varied inversely with the percentage of African American students. The findings further suggested that achievement tended to decline as the number of African American students increased in schools. However, this decline was not found to be statistically significant. Unlike Matzen (1965), St. John and Lewis (1971) found that European American children living in racially changing neighborhoods in Boston were likely to perform lower on tests and that the greater the percentage of African American students in the elementary grades, in earlier grades, the lower the later achievement of European Americans in reading and mathematics, even when socioeconomic status is controlled. Jencks and Brown (1975) conducted a study that measured the effect of racial composition of schools on academic achievement. They used data gathered in 1965 from 359 northern elementary schools and 154 northern high schools from the Coleman Report. The researchers concluded that racially balanced elementary schools may have modest effects on both African American and European American students' achievement test scores. Research suggested that on the average, attending a predominantly European American elementary school increased African American students' test scores by 0.215 standard deviations, and that if African Americans gained this much, relative to the European American students, between first and sixth grades, the test score gap between African American and European Americans would narrow by 21 percent.

The National Assessment of Educational Progress studies achievement changes in relation to school racial composition. Findings indicated that seventeen-year olds in the Southeast decreased in achievement, but those who attended schools that were 10% European American showed an increase in achievement. Nine-year-old African Americans in the north showed a decrease of 3.5%. Those who attended up to 2.5% European American schools in 1972–73 gained 2.5 percentage points over 1969–70 (Weinberg, 1983). A second study, conducted by Narot (1973) at the Harvard University's National Opinion Research Center, found that in newly desegregated southern high schools, the achievement scores among African American students tended to be lower in schools where African Americans made up less than 20% of the student body. As previously stated, there has been a limited body of research concerning the effects of desegregation on the academic achievement of European American children. Data retrieved in the 1960s from the Equality of Educational Opportunity Survey indicated that verbal achievement test scores of European American students declined as the proportion of African Americans in schools increased, especially where schools had an African American majority (Coleman, 1966). However, this relationship did not exist when socioeconomic levels were controlled. Narot (1973) found that when students' social class levels were controlled, achievement scores for European American students in the tenth grade increased as the proportion of African Americans in their schools increased. Narot noted that for European American male tenth-grade students, and all fifth-grade European Americans, there was no significant relationship between racial composition and achievement scores.

Rossell and Hawley (1983) contend that there are not enough African American teachers to provide minority students the sense of being integrated into the school. According to Mahard and Crain (1978), two main findings have appeared consistently in large-scale desegregation studies. First, minority students in predominantly European American schools score higher on achievement tests. Second, this factor appears to result from predominantly European American schools having student bodies with higher socioeconomic status. These findings suggest that the best desegregation plan is one that creates predominantly European American schools using European American students from relative affluent families. Bridge, Judd and Mock (1979), reviewed several major studies from large samples of schools and found that there was no relationship between the achievement test scores of European American students and school racial composition. These researchers also found that with one exception, African American students' achievement test scores were higher in predominately European American schools. However, one researcher (Winkler, 1975) found a negative effect on students from African American elementary schools. Many researchers challenged his findings because of the lack of rigor in his instrument. Many of his selected studies were cross-sectional and utilized measures of family background as substitutes for pretests. It has long been contended that the nation's public elementary schools are gateways to equalizing opportunities for minority students can become reality. Therefore, this social institution is viewed by many as the primary source for improving the life chances of African American and disadvantaged children. However, as Kozol (1996) noted in his book *Amazing Grace*, schools are not equal. Society does not provide equal opportunities for its darker-skin children. In the 1970s and 1980s, extensive research was conducted on the relationship between attending segregated schools and the achievement test scores of students by race. Prior to the 1954 *Brown* decision, school desegregation as a variable and its impact upon the academic achievement of African American children was rarely researched. This section will examine and elaborate research findings relevant to the relationship between desegregated schooling and academic achievement.

The possible educational consequences of busing for school desegregation have received limited attention in the literature. The most comprehensive study of the effects of the policy of mandated busing for integration involved a sample of 450 schools. This study was conducted by Davis (1973) as part of the southern schools research of Robert Crain and associates. Davis investigated the effects of busing on tension in the school, student morale, race relations, and academic achievement. This study concluded that there was no evidence to support the contention that attending a neighborhood school has any effect, positive or negative, on a school's achievement levels. Longitudinal data from desegregated school systems in Chapel Hill, North Carolina; Evanston, Illinois; Goldsboro, North Carolina; Louisville, Kentucky; Riverside, California; Washington, D.C.; and White Plains, New York indicated that school desegregation had had no negative consequences for European American students. In studies of the effect of busing on academic achievement, findings indicated that there were no significant differences in achievement between bused and non-bused students (St. John, 1975).

Purl and Dawson (1971) summarized the findings from the Riverside desegregation project. The researchers found that after seven years of desegregation, the achievement of kindergarten and first-grade African American students increased consistently. However, the students in grade two exhibited no specific trends, while those in the third grade declined slightly. The increase in academic performance was attributed to improvements in the quality of teaching. A few studies are available on the academic progress of European American students bused to schools in low socioeconomic neighborhoods. In Shaker Heights, Ohio European American students in grade four who were reassigned to a majority African American school gained more than European American students in the rest of the system. In Evanston, self-selected European American students who were bused to previously all-African-American schools had achievement test scores above the national average (St. John, 1975). O'Riley (1970) reported on two studies similar that of St. John. One study, conducted in New York, found that European American students transported to a school with an African American majority made less academic progress than European American students who attended majority European American schools (Wrightstone et al., 1966). In a second study of reverse busing in Rochester, New York, no significant differences between the two groups of European American students were found except that fourth- grade students who were transferred to urban schools showed statistically significantly higher achievement test scores in mathematics and vocabulary.

Another study conducted by Mayer (1973) studied a school system in Goldsboro, North Carolina in which there was busing of African American and European American students. After more than two years of busing, significant increases for African American elementary students were noted in the area of mathematics, for those students who were involved in desegregation longer. These findings indicated that both African American and European American students showed a significant increase in mathematics and verbal skills. St. John (1975) found that in most desegregation studies, there was no conclusive evidence that desegregation was directly related to improved achievement. However, the Goldsboro study shows evidence of increased performance in mathematics. In an effort to determine the extent to which busing for the purpose of desegregation influences the academic performance of students in general and African American students specifically, Hayes (1981) investigated the grade- point averages of forty African American male and female students who were bused to a suburban high school. Two aspects of the grade- point averages were investigated: the grade-point average attained by bused African American students in their former schools during the year prior to busing (1974–1975), and the grade-point average achieved in the fall quarter of 1975–1976 after being bused to a suburban high school. The control group consisted of forty African American male and female students who were not bused for desegregation, but attended the same school during the fall quarter of the 1975–76 school year. Similar comparisons of the grade-point average for the non-bused students were made between the two periods. The purpose of this study was to determine if any significant change in grade-point average occurred for a group of forty bused students between the year preceding the busing, 1974–1975, and the fall quarter of 1975–1976, the first year of court ordered busing. The findings from this study were not supported by previous research. Previous research indicated that there were no negative effects on European American students, but there were increases in achievement for African American students who attended desegregated schools. The grade-point averages for bused students were significantly lower for the fall quarter of the 1974–1975 school year (1.49) than for the 1974–75 school year (2.41). The data revealed that grade-point averages of non-bused students during the same period of comparison were lower.

Phillips and Bianchi (1975) examined the effect of achievement on closing an all-African-American school and busing its 353 students to predominantly European American middle-class schools in Nevada City, California. For the purposes of comparison, they used a matched sample of all African American schools as a control. After seven months, the bused African American students scored higher than the segregated African American students in two of three reading areas tested. However, after two years there was no difference in performance. The aptitude scores of the desegregated students increased by more than two years and declined for their segregated counterparts. In an investigation of the effects of desegregation on academic achievement on elementary students in Grand Rapids, Michigan, Schellenberg, and Halteman (1976) matched sixty-eight pairs of urban elementary students. The researchers analyzed the test scores over a period of two years. There were no achievement differences in reading or mathematics between bused and non-bused African American students. The majority of investigations regarding the achievement of students in desegregated schools suggest that the levels of academic achievement generally improved for African American students in desegregated schools (Teele, Jackson, & Mayo, 1967; Weinberg, 1970), while the performance of European American students did not decline. Lemke (1979) studied the effects of school desegregation on academic achievement in Peoria, Illinois. His sample consisted of European American students attending previously segregated African American schools, bused European American students attending integrated and segregated European American schools, African American students attending segregated African American schools, and bused African American students attending segregated European American schools. African Americans who were bused out of segregated African American schools to majority European American schools tended to achieve at a higher level than African Americans who were bused from similar schools to schools that were minority European American. European Americans in predominantly African American neighborhood schools achieved at levels higher than African American students at the same school. These findings contradict those of the 1966 Coleman Report.

In an effort to determine if significant change in grade point average occurred for a group of forty bused African American children, Pride and Woodard (1985) studied the relationship between busing and academic achievement in the Metro schools in Nashville, Tennessee. The results of this study indicated that the percentage of students of the opposite race in a given school was not related to academic achievement. Specifically, the findings indicated that the number of schools attended was not related to success, that attendance in court-ordered schools was just as likely to stimulate improved scores as attendance in non-court-ordered schools, and that and the percentage of students of the opposite race in a student's grade was not related to performance on tests.

SOCIOECONOMIC LEVEL AND THE ACHIEVEMENT GAP

A 2002 study by the Economic Policy Institute (EPI) conducted by Lee and Burkman, found that the cognitive abilities of children who enter kindergarten are quite high and that socioeconomic status, more than any other factor, accounts for differences in cognition among these children. The researchers found that socioeconomic background was more important than race/ethnicity, family educational level (Lee, and Burkam, 2002). According to Suzanne Weiss, (2003), the EPI analysis of data from the United States Department of Education's Early Childhood Education Longitudinal Study Kindergarten Cohort found the following:

> There are significant differences by race and ethnicity in test scores as children begin kindergarten.
>
> Race and ethnicity are highly correlated with socio-economic status.
>
> Family structure and educational expectations are strongly correlated socio-economic status, race/ethnicity and young children's test scores.
>
> Socioeconomic status is highly correlated to cognition.
>
> Students of low socio-economic status begin school in systematically lower-quality elementary schools than their more advantaged counterparts, reinforcing the inequities that develop even before children enter school. (Weiss, p. 2)

In another study focusing on the racial/ethnic achievement, Hedges and Nowell (1999) sought to determine the degree to which racial differences can be attributed to social class differences between African American and European American students. They examined the trends in the achievement gap between the two groups over a thirty-year period. The researchers analyzed data from a national sample (1965–1996). They concluded that the racial gap was extensive, but decreasing slowly, and that about one-third of the gap in test scores was attributed to racial differences in social class. Hedges and Nowell also found that the gap has narrowed since 1965; however, the rate of decline has decreased since 1972. Additionally, findings from their study indicated that European American and African American children were becoming more equal in performance at the lower end of the test distribution. This was not the case at the top of the distribution. In fact, African American students were practically non-existent.

Many have long contended that African American and European children live in two distinctly different realities; therefore, their cultural experiences differ. According to this thesis, the African American child is generally exposed to values different from those in the Euro-centered public schools. Some believe that African American children continue to be left behind in classrooms that are dominated by typical middle-class curricula. The failure of schools to develop curricula that reflect the values of non-middle class children frequently result in poor academic performance. This poor performance frequently results from a disconnect between the school's environment and the needs and interests of African American children. It has been argued that standardized test often fail to assess African American children's ability to learn and that they measure what these individuals have internalized about the dominant European culture.

As Haskins and Rouse (2005) noted:

> By the time black and Hispanic children reach kindergarten, they are on average already far behind their more advantaged peers in reading and math readiness. Such disparities in achievement persist or even increase during the school years. Educational programs for parents and preschool education programs for children have the potential to narrow these disparities by at least half. (p. 1)

Bias in standardized tests has been a topic of debate among scholars for decades. As far back as the 1920s, African American sociologist, Allison Davis (1948,) examined the relationship between culture and performance on intelligence test, and noted that the relative success of two individual solving given problems on a standardized test depends not just on innate ability but also upon how familiar the individuals are with cultural situations and symbols, their relative training with similar problems and relative strength of third motivation.

Davis lived a privileged life and was educated at Williams College, Harvard, and the University of Chicago. While teaching African American children in a rural Virginia town in 1925, he saw firsthand the relationship between social class and academic achievement. He commented, "teaching in the standard manner made no sense to these poor and poorly schooled rural blacks. I decided that I didn't know anything to teach them since our backgrounds were so different, yet I wanted to do something to affect such students." Davis (1939) contended that in order to improve the life chances of African American students:

> We must make it possible for a much larger proportion of Negroes to obtain the kinds of occupations, income, education, and legal protection necessary for middle class training...and we must learn to do a new kind of remedial

work with individuals, in which we direct them toward new class-goals and show them the techniques for reaching these goals. (pp. 273–274)

Davis (1951) believed that aptitude tests appear to measure only the problem-solving skills that stress verbal aptitude and the ability to solve abstract problems. As he stated, "The middle-class may be expected to prove superior on the present tests, because this group has had more training on the specific test problems or on closely related problems" (p. 28). Middle-class students are typically better prepared to solve these problems than their lower-class counterparts. Therefore, middle-class students are expected to perform better on standardized tests. Cultural bias in an intelligence test may occur for several reasons. As Davis stipulated, test items in the past have frequently been validated in such a way as to eliminate precisely those items on which students in the lowest socioeconomic groups tend to perform best. Therefore, the measure of an item's validity is dependent upon how well it is able to distinguish successfully between students of known superior and known inferior ability. Specifically, any item on which the performance of the lowest third of the students is as good or superior to the performance of the highest third of the students is automatically eliminated from the test itself. The effect of this approach is the "lowest third" of the students, those who will primarily fall into the lowest socioeconomic groups, will not be allowed to show, in the final test, any of the activities at which they are superior or equal.

As Davis (1951) suggested, performance on standardized tests depends not only upon the possession of certain linguistic skills, but also upon the choice of words and situations used in these tests. Typically, the words and situations used to deal with concepts that are most closely associated with a middle-class child's environment, are missing from the background of child from a low socioeconomic background. As Davis and Eells (1953) noted:

> Pupils coming from the top and bottom social strata live in cultures which, though alike in certain fundamental American activities, are yet different in many other cultural habits and motives. At a great many points, therefore, their cultures differ with respect to the types of problems, they teach each group to recognize and to solve. (Davis & Eells, 1953, p. 27)

The population on which a standardized test is normed may explain why African Americans frequently fail to achieve satisfactory levels of performance. Aptitude and achievement tests are not cultural free. As emphasized in the Coleman Report (1966), the degree to which a child has assimilated a culture appropriate to modern life in the United States is emphasized by standardized tests. Failure to perform satisfactorily on these tests may be best viewed as the as being indicative of the social gaps and inequities suffered by African American children. Several studies have shown that academic achievement is highly correlated with social class.

Rist (1970) reported the results of an observational study on one class of socially disadvantaged students during their kindergarten, first- and second-grade years. His study showed how the kindergarten teacher placed the children in reading groups that reflected the racial composition of the class, and how these groups persisted throughout the first several years of elementary school. The manner in which the teachers interacted with the different groups became an important influence on the children's achievement. Rist reached this conclusion after examining the relationship between the caste system in the classroom and the caste system of the wider society.

Coleman (1966) found that school percentage European American bears little relation to verbal achievement that is independent of the influence of individual and school social background. According to his findings, the most important variable in showing the strongest relationship to academic achievement of African American children was social class. The Coleman Report found that the higher performance of African American children attending schools with a high percentage of European American children was not attributed to the racial composition of the school but to better educational preparation and higher aspirations among European American students.

In sum, the analysis of the Coleman data suggested that European American students appeared to be less affected by the quality of their schools (school characteristics) than their African American counterparts. Coleman suggested that improving school quality will have the most significant effect on academic achievement for disadvantaged students. The report stated:

1. For each group (eight ethnic groups were examined), by far, the largest variation in student achievement lies within, and not between schools.
2. Comparisons of schools, by school differences in achievement, at the beginning of grade one with later years indicated that only a small portion of it is the result of school factors, in contrast to family background differences between communities.
3. There is indirect evidence that school factors are more important in affecting the achievement of minority students; among African American students. This appears especially so in the South. This leads to a different sensitivity to school variations, with the lowest achieving schools minority groups showing the highest sensitivity (Bliss, 1991).

After the publication of his report, many researchers began to question Coleman's findings that suggested that school characteristics (class size, quality of textbooks, physical plant, teachers' experiences, library size, and other variables), had almost no effect on student achievement. However, four years after the Coleman Report, Guthrie (1970) analyzed the results of nineteen studies completed prior to 1970 and concluded that school characteristics had more of an effect on student achievement than Coleman suggested. According to Guthrie (1970):

> The strongest findings by far are those which relate to the number and quality of the professional staff, particularly teachers. Fifteen of the 22 studies we reviewed find teacher characteristics such as verbal ability, and type of academic preparation, degree status, job satisfaction, and employment status (tenured/untenured), to be significantly associated With one or more measures of student performance. (Guthrie, 1970, p. 32)

Armor (1972) reanalyzed Coleman's data and found that the verbal ability of European American students in majority African American schools is as low or lower than that of African American classmates. Findings suggested that the low socioeconomic status of these students and perhaps that of their classmates is primarily responsible for their low achievement. McPartland (1967) also reexamined parts of the Coleman Report data to separate the effects of race from social class upon achievement. The study concluded that there is a positive correlation between racial composition and achievement test sores, no matter what the racial composition of the school may be. The researcher proposed two reasons for the inconsistency between their findings and those of the Coleman Report: (a) the statistical techniques used in the earlier study tended to confuse social class and race; and (b) the Coleman Report in the regression analysis used the school rather than the classroom as the unit of analysis.

Klein and Eshel (1977) studied the initial effects of desegregation during an eight month period in three high schools located in a southern urban area: one recently desegregated; one that was 100% African American, and the other virtually all-European-American. The African American students performed better in the desegregated schools. However, when parental occupation, parental education, and family size, were controlled, this superiority disappeared. Klein concluded that the integrated school setting is neither educationally deleterious nor beneficial for African American students. He also observed that the academic achievement of matched groups of segregated African American students and integrated European American students did not differ significantly.

Wilson (1967) completed a study in Richmond, California in which he concluded that the racial composition of the school, while tending to favor African American students in integrated schools, does not have an effect as significant as social class composition of the school. Wilson also found that the social-class composition of the school had more of an effect on African American than European American students. He noted that there were very few African American students in the sample from predominately European American schools or from predominately upper-class schools. This factor indicated that the number of African Americans in the sample was too small to test the relationship of social class and race in schools of varying racial compositions. In addition to the small numbers, there were additional limitations to this study:

1. The first-grade test scores were not available for all members of members of the sample; therefore the instability of the sample impacted the findings.
2. Measures of school social class and parental social class were poorly defined.
3. Regression analysis may have underestimated the relationship between school racial composition and achievement.

When racial composition as well as socioeconomic level is held constant, there is no evidence that the percentage of European Americans enrolled in schools has a significant influence on the achievement of African American students (Laurent, 1969). African American students who remained in segregated classes in desegregated schools experienced no academic growth. These findings suggest that segregated classes may be less harmful to African American's achievement if they occur in mostly European American schools rather than mainly African American schools. In a study of the relationship between socioeconomic status and academic achievement of African American and European American students, Purl (1969) found the relationship to be significant. There were significant variations in scores of African American and European American children. There were also significant variations in scores that had little to do with socioeconomic level. Purl also examined two minority groups (African Americans and Mexican Americans) in four schools. She found that a negative relationship existed between socioeconomic status and achievement. Purl suggested that her findings have made competing explanations, such as school environment and teaching style, worthy of exploration.

Some studies have found that the beneficial effects of attending desegregated schools extend beyond in-school academic achievement. Crain (1971) found a significant impact on achievement scores of African Americans who attended desegregated schools, even allowing for socioeconomic differences. Crain suggested that African American students learn what it means to live in an integrated society, which stimulates African American students to higher achievement. Further analysis indicated that, in addition to improving their academic achievements, African American students in desegregated settings were likely to attend college and enter occupations usually closed to African Americans.

Shaw (1973) found a progressive decline in academic achievement in the New York City Public Schools. As Shaw noted, children from low socioeconomic areas also tend to fall farther behind in achievement than their peers. In one large district in New York City, the average third-grade child was found to be behind by one year in reading, by almost two years in grade six, and by two and one-half years by grade eight. A number of researchers (Jencks, Smith, Acland, Bane, Cohen, Gintis, Heyns, & Michelson, 1972; Klein & Eshe, 1977) have stressed the need to teach educational norms and values to lower socioeconomic students. Pettigrew and Pajonas (1964) suggested that a proportion of 60% to 80% middle class students should optimally promote positive integration. According to Mahard and Crain (1978), in many instances, desegregation is helpful because lower socio- economic African American students are brought together with higher in-come European American students. This benefits lower socioeconomic students for several reasons. When there are high-income students in the classroom, the teacher will maintain a faster pace and cover more material. Additionally, teachers will set higher standards and will expect better performance from African American students. The authors also noted that they suspect that even the best teachers in segregated, low-income, or African American schools come to expect less of students. If a school is known as a low-income African American school, achievement is expected to be low, and low performance becomes a self-fulfilling prophecy. Crain and Mahard further contended that low-income students tend naturally to fall in with the way higher income students in a classroom do things.

SUMMARY

A review of relevant desegregation research indicated that desegregation has improved the academic achievement of African American students. Of the numerous studies reviewed in this chapter, only a few give indications that placing African American children in desegregated schools might lessen their rate of academic achievement. There is virtually no evidence that desegregation lowers the achievement levels of European American children. Educators continue to debate and examine why children from higher socioeconomic families perform better academically than children who live in poverty. As Wise and Gendler (1989) noted, this disparity is related to the types of schools that children attend and not just their socioeconomic backgrounds. The authors found that most advantaged children are likely to attend schools that are clean, well- staffed, have up to date books, and state-of-the-art technology. The exact opposite was found to be the case for disadvantaged children. It is the contention of some educators that, in order to improve student performance, resources should be redistributed to reflect existing imbalances.

Although funding is important, money cannot buy a quality education, the financial resources of a school district will affect school quality (Wise & Gendler, 1989). It is important to realize that equity in the distribution of resources will not automatically result in equally outcomes in terms of academic achievement. Money cannot buy a quality education. It is important to realize that equity in the distribution of resources will not automatically result in equally outcomes in terms of academic achievement. Nevertheless, funding is important. The financial resources of a school district will affect school quality (Wise & Gendler, 1989).

Weiss (2003) summarized findings from a report from the North Carolina First initiative, which enumerated specific changes that schools should employ to reduce the achievement gap. These were:

> Expand high quality, academically focused early childhood education to all children at risk of school failure.
>
> Ensure well prepared and experienced teachers teach Black children.
>
> Reduce class size in the elementary grades.
>
> Ensure that Black students are equitably represented across curriculum tracks in high schools.
>
> Bridge home and school culture by adapting teaching and disciple practices appropriate to students' backgrounds.
>
> Demand success by holding both schools and students accountable.
>
> Support students with individual tutoring, more comprehensive reforms, summer programs and follow-up assistance.
>
> Desegregate schools and programs within schools. (Weiss, 2003, p. 4)

CHAPTER 6

ACHIEVEMENT GAPS AND RESEGREGATION IN NORFOLK

An Empirical Analysis

Education: a debt due from present to future generations.
—George Peabody, 1852

In 1987, the Norfolk Public School System had a student population of 35,474. The system had 37 elementary schools, eight junior high schools, and five elementary schools. There were 17,117 students enrolled in the city's elementary schools, 18,808 at the junior and senior high levels and 2,200 teachers. Additionally there was a vocational-technical school for high school students, a vocational training center for adults, two schools for the handicapped, and three alternative education schools. The district's fourth grade population for the 1986–87 academic year was 2,626. The majority of the students are in school for 180 days.

As a means of achieving unitary school systems, the Norfolk School District implemented using a desegregation strategy. Mandated busing was intended to help African American children close the achievement gap between African American and European American children. A study of the achievement gap between African American and European American children was conducted to determine the effects of the policy of mandated

Narrowing the Achievement Gap in a (Re)Segregated Urban School District, pages 79–111
Copyright © 2009 by Information Age Publishing
79

busing on the overall achievement test scores of fourth-grade students in the Norfolk Public Schools.

This study was designed to ascertain the answers to the following research questions:

1. What are the effects of busing for the purposes of desegregation on the overall achievement scores of African American students?
2. What are the effects of busing for the purposes of desegregation on the overall achievement scores of European American students?
3. What are the effects of the policy of mandated busing upon the achievement gap between African American and European American fourth-grade students?

The methodology utilized in this study was descriptive research, which is concerned with hypothesis formulation and testing, the relationship between non-manipulative variables, and the development of generalizations. The statistical data were gathered from the test results of fourth-grade students through the administration of the Science Research Associates Assessment Survey Series (SRA).

DATA SOURCES

Relevant research data were obtained from the Norfolk Public Schools Department of Research, Testing and Statistics. The name, gender, race, test results, and school attended for each student were obtained for the 1986 and 1987 SRA achievement test. The 1986 test results represent the achievement scores of the fourth grade students during the busing year and the 1987 scores reflected the test scores for the non-busing year. The reading, language arts, and mathematics sections of the Science Research Associates Assessment Series were administered to all third grade students in April 1986. These students represent the selected fourth grade sample. The SRA Level 4 was administered one year later to the selected fourth grade students. Students in grade three during the 1985–86 school year were attending school under the mandated busing policy. These same (matched set) students were promoted to the fourth grade during the 1986–87 school year, after the elimination of mandated busing for desegregation. Another source of data was *The Report by School Year* (1987). Data relevant to school expenditures and racial distribution of teachers and students; were obtained from this report. Specifics related to teachers' salaries, substitute teacher expenditures, library books, ages of school buildings, student/teacher ratios, percentage of teachers with advanced degrees, and average class size were obtained from the Virginia Department of Education and the United States Department of Education.

School desegregation studies should separate the influence of socioeconomic status from the influence of race on achievement test scores. Socioeconomic indicators for individual students could not be obtained in this sample; therefore, school-income level indicators were collected from Census Tracts for the city of Norfolk. These data were collected from the United States Bureau of Commerce, Bureau of the Census, Census Tracts, Norfolk Census of Population and Housing (Norfolk Census Tracts, 1980). The specific data collected were mean household incomes of the neighborhood school zones. The results from all the collected data provided a means of comparing statistical differences in overall achievement test scores of fourth-grade students during and after the elimination of the mandated busing policy.

The dependent variable in this study is the achievement scores on the SRA Achievement Test of African American and European American students from selected elementary schools. The primary independent variable in this study is mandated busing within the Norfolk Public Schools District. Secondary independent variables investigated were: school income level; school racial composition, student and teacher; school expenditures, instructional, substitute, and teacher salaries; the number of library books; age of the school building; student/teacher ratio; percentage of students with advanced degrees; average class size, and housing patterns (students attending a particular school on the basis of housing patterns rather than busing). The above variables were collected for the 1985–86 (busing) and 1986–87 (non-busing school years). The differences between these school characteristics were computed using multiple regression statistical tests.

DESCRIPTION OF 1986–87 STUDENT POPULATION

The average per pupil expenditure level in schools with 50–90% African American enrollment was $1,433.08 or 96.3% of the system-wide average. The 8,800 average daily membership of these schools, represented 47% of the city's elementary students and 4.8% of the district's total expenditures for elementary education. On the other hand, the average per pupil expenditure level for the non-minority group schools was $1,374.00 and reflected 31% of total expenditures. Additionally, of Norfolk's 1,127 elementary teachers, 18% had 0–5 years experience; 34%, 6–10 years; 21% 11–15 and 28%, more than 16 years. Approximately 24% of the total teaching force held advanced degrees. The district's teacher racial distribution was 57% European American and 43% minority.

The methodology of this study involved grouping the city's 37 elementary schools into three categories (a) 10 target schools comprising over 90% African American enrollment, (b) mixed schools comprising 10–50% European American enrollment, and (c) predominately European American schools comprising over 50% European American enrollment. The average expenditure per pupil in the target schools was $1,824 or 122.9% of the system wide elementary average. The 3,487 average daily memberships of the target schools, representing 18.8% of the students, had $6,378.19 spent on them or 23.1% of the total expenditures on elementary education. The average expenditure per pupil in the schools with 50–90% African American enrollment was $1,433.08 or 96.3% of the system wide average. The 8,800 average daily memberships of these schools, representing 47% of the city's elementary students, had $12,611 spent on them or 4.8% of the total expenditures on elementary education. The average expenditures per pupil in this group were $1,374.00 or 92% of the system wide average. The 6,226 average daily memberships, representing 33.7% of the city's elementary students had $8,548 spent on them or 31.15% of the total expenses on elementary education.

The average teacher salary was $25,000. Of Norfolk's 1,127 elementary teachers, 18% had 0–5 years experience; 34%, 6–10 years; 21%, 11–15%; and 28% more than 16 years. Additionally, 24% of the total teaching force held an advanced degree. The racial composition of the systems teachers was 67% European American and 43% minority.

SAMPLE

The fourth-grade student population of the Norfolk School District for the 1986–87 school year consisted of approximately 2,200 students. Of this total, 900 students received supplemental instruction under the systems Chapter 1 program. This program provides instruction to students who have been identified as low achievers in the areas of language arts and mathematics. Under the Chapter 1 program, funds are provided to state and local education agencies to assist them in providing compensatory education programs for disadvantaged students. Seventy-three of the students in this sample participated in the Chapter 1 program in grade four. Only students in grades four, five, and six were eligible to participate in the Chapter 1 program; therefore, none of the students in this sample participated in the program during the desegregated school year.

To determine the effects of resegregation on the achievement gap between African American and European American fourth grade students, subjects were randomly selected from eleven Norfolk elementary schools.

The selected sample was comprised of 98 African American males, 129 European American males, 105 African American females, and 99 European American females. The African American students in this sample attended 23 different elementary schools during the desegregation period (Table 6.1) and nine different schools after resegregation (Table 6.2). As shown in Tables 6.3 and 6.4 the European American students attended 18 different schools during the desegregation year and only 8 after resegregation. Additionally, 48% of African American students were bused during the desegregation period, as compared to 33% of their European American counterparts (Tables 6.5 and 6.6).

TABLE 6.1   Schools Attended by NPS Grade Four African Americans During Desegregation

School	Frequency	Percent
8	19	9.4
15	4	2.0
21	1	0.5
22	38	18.7
23	13	6.4
26	11	5.4
28	32	15.8
29	1	0.5
30	4	2.0
34	3	1.5
35	10	4.9
41	12	5.9
42	3	1.5
45	2	1.0
46	9	4.4
49	1	0.5
51	2	1.0
53	13	0.5
54	3	6.4
56	2	1.5
59	12	1.0
60	5	5.9
68	2	2.5
114		1.0
Total	203	100.00

TABLE 6.2 Schools Attended by Grade Four NPS African American Students During Resegregation

School	Frequency	Percent
8	42	20.7
22	40	19.7
28	38	18.7
41	15	7.4
46	29	14.3
51	10	4.9
54	7	3.4
56	10	4.9
60	12	5.9
Total	203	100.0

TABLE 6.3 Schools Attended by European American Students During Desegregation

School	Frequency	Percent
8	5	2.2
22	7	3.1
23	3	1.3
26	4	1.8
28	46	20.2
29	9	3.9
34	4	1.8
35	18	7.9
41	40	17.5
42	2	.9
46	16	7.0
49	1	.4
51	13	5.7
54	19	8.3
56	19	8.3
68	15	6.6
106	2	.9
114	5	2.2
Total	228	100.00

TABLE 6.4 Schools Attended by European American Students During Resegregation

School	Frequency	Percent
8	1	0.4
28	45	19.7
29	4	1.8
41	48	21.1
46	41	18.0
51	16	7.0
54	27	11.8
56	25	11.0
68	21	9.2
Total	228	100.0

TABLE 6.5 Bused and Non-Bused African American Students–Desegregation

	Frequency	Percent
Bused	98	48.3
Non-Bused	105	51.7
Total	203	100.0

TABLE 6.6 Bused and Non-Bused European American Students–Desegregation

	Frequency	Percent
Bused	75	32.9
Non-Bused	153	67.1
Total	228	100.0

FINDINGS

Presented in Table 6.7 are the number of students, mean scores, and selected statistics for the T-test. The T-test statistical procedure was performed to determine if a statistically significant difference ($p < .05$) existed between the SRA composite test scores of African American students during the existence of the policy of mandated busing for desegregation and after the return elimination of the policy. The mean score for African American students during the 1985–86 busing year was 52.57; however, the mean for these same students was 47.15 for the 1986–87, after busing was eliminated. This mean difference of 5.41 represented a decline in the achievement test scores of African American students following the elimination of busing mandated for integration. As indicated, the mean difference was statistically significant ($p < .05$). Research findings (Tables 6.8 and 6.9) indicated that both male and female students performed significantly higher on the achievement tests during the year of mandated busing for desegregation. The mean score for African American females during the busing year was 54.77 and 50.26 for African American males. However, after the elimination of mandated busing

TABLE 6.7   African American Students Busing and Post-Busing T-test Results Grade Achievement Gaps and Resegregation in Norfolk

Grade		Number of cases	Mean	*t* value	df	2-tail
3	Bused	203	52.57	4.30	202	.000
4	Non-bused	203	47.15			

TABLE 6.8   T-test Results for Desegregation/Resegregation Achievement Gap for African American Females

Grade		Number of cases	Mean	*t* value	df	2-tail
3	Bused	105	54.77	2.38	104	.019
4	Non-bused	105	50.06			

TABLE 6.9   T-test Results for Desegregation/Resegregation Achievement Gap for African American Males

Grade		Number of cases	Mean	*t* value	df	2-tail
3	Bused	98	50.26	3.99	97	.000
4	Non-bused	98	44.10			

for integration, the mean score for African American females was 50.04 and 44.10 for African American males. The mean difference in achievement test scores appeared to be statistically significant ($p < .05$) for both sexes. The findings suggest that that African American males and African American females performed better on the test prior to the elimination of the policy of mandated busing for desegregation. Further analysis of data indicated that the scores of African American males declined more after the end of mandated desegregation than their African American female counterparts.

Historically, African American females have performed at significantly higher levels than African American males on standardized tests. The findings from this study tend to support this. As indicated, the T-test yielded a significant value, which leads to the conclusion that African American students performed better on achievement tests during the existence of the policy of mandated busing for desegregation. Based upon these findings, multiple regression statistical models were selected for further analysis. In this research study, multiple linear regression analysis was employed to determine the effects of selected school characteristics on the achievement test scores of African American students. Data relevant to school characteristics during the existence of mandated busing for school integration and after its elimination were collected for each individual student in the sample.

Specific data collected per student were: school income level, instructional expenditures, school racial composition for teachers and students, average teachers' salary, percentage of teachers with advanced degrees, number of library books per school, age of the school boiling boiler, average class size, student teacher ratio, and substitute teacher expenditures. These data represent the independent variables utilized to compute differences between school characteristics during the existence of the desegregation policy and after its elimination. Multiple regression was undertaken to determine if variance in achievement test scores could be attributed to the selected school characteristics resulting from the mandated desegregation policy change.

African American Students, School Characteristics and the Achievement Gap

As shown in Table 6.10 the adjusted R square for the eleven school characteristics was .08293 with an F value of 2.6605. These results suggested that only 8% of the variance could be accounted for by the eleven selected school characteristics The F value suggested that this 8% variance was statistically significant ($p < .05$); therefore, a linear relationship existed between the achievement test scores and school characteristics.

Further analysis indicated (Table 6.11) that three school characteristics were significant in explaining the variance in test scores. As indicated, the average school income level is positively related to test scores for African American students. As the income level of school increased, the achievement test scores of African Americans increased. The variable, student percentage of African American students had a T value of –2.47. These results suggested that as the percentage of African American students increased in a given school, the achievement test scores for all African Americans declined. As indicated by these findings, a statistically significant negative relationship existed between school percentage of African American students and the achievement test scores of these students. There also appeared to be a negative relationship between average teacher salary and achievement

TABLE 6.10 Multiple Regression Statistics for All African American Students

Multiple R	.36451
R Squared	.13287
Adjusted Square	.08293
Standard Error	17.36995

Analysis of Variance

	DF	Sum of Squares	Mean Squares
Regression	11	8830.01134	802.72830
Residual	191	57627.62413	301.71531

F = 2.66055   Significance of F = .0034

TABLE 6.11 Multiple Regression Statistics for All African American Students

Variables	Beta	T	Significance of T
Percentage African American students	–.45846	–2.474	.0142
Average teacher salary	.21297	–2.370	.0188
Age of school building	–.07862	–1.093	.2758
Substitute expenditures	.02849	.296	.7677
School income	.37166	3.745	.0002
Instructional expenditures	.19660	1.846	.0665
Percentage with advanced degrees	.02444	.216	.8290
Percentage African American teachers	.09333	.854	.3943
Average class size	–.02204	–.165	.2808
Student–Teacher ratio	–.15094	–1.082	.0707
Library books	.25445	1.818	.1250
(Constant)		1.541	.1250

test scores of African American students. Findings indicated that average teacher salary has a statistically significant ($p < .05$) T value of −2.370. Accordingly, as the average teacher's salary of a given school increased, the test scores of African American students tended to decrease.

African American Males

The results in Table 6.12 indicated that the adjusted R square for the eleven independent variables was .08912. This value indicated that approximately 9% of the total variance in the test scores of African American males

TABLE 6.12   Multiple Regression Statistics for African American Males

Multiple R	.43865
R Squared	.19242
Adjusted Square	.08912
Standard Error	14.95597

Analysis of Variance

	DF	Sum of Squares	Mean Squares
Regression	11	4583.38170	416.67106
Residual	86	19236.57749	223.68113

F = 1.86279   Significance of F = .0557

TABLE 6.13   Multiple Regression Statistics for African American Males

Variables	Beta	T	Significance of T
Percentage African American students	−.62075	−2.153	.0341
Substitute expenditures	−.22898	−1.512	.1341
Average teacher salary	−.39992	−2.752	.0072
Age of school building	−.10016	−.881	.3810
School income	.34693	2.278	.0252
Instructional expenditures	−.01840	.144	.9094
Percentage with advanced degrees	.24964	1.445	.1520
Percentage African American teachers	.41997	2.503	.0142
Library books	−.26565	−1.289	.2010
Student–Teacher ratio	−.16429	−.794	.4295
Average class size	−.04165	−.198	.8436
(Constant)			.0223

may be attributed to changes in school characteristics. The F value of 1.862 suggested that there was no statistically significant linear relationship between the achievement test scores and the eleven school characteristics for African American males. As indicated in Table 6.13, statistical results suggested that the percentage of African American students in schools appeared to have a negative effect upon the achievement of African American males. School student percentage African American has a T value of −2.153; therefore, it was statistically significant ($p < .05$). In explaining variance in test scores. Analysis of data found that as the percentage of African American students declined in a given school, the achievement test scores for African Americans increased.

The percentage of African American teachers in school also appeared to be statistically significant ($p < .05$) in explaining variance in test scores. The percentage of African American teachers in a school had a T-value of 2.503. Accordingly, as the percentage of African American teachers increased in a given school, the achievement test scores of African American males increased. The school income level also appeared to be statistically significant ($p < .05$) in explaining the variance in achievement test scores of African American males. As shown in Table 6.13, school income level has a T-value of 2.278. These data suggested that as school income level increased, the achievement test scores of African American males increased. Unlike the above two variables, average teachers' salary appeared to have a negative effect upon the achievement test scores of African American males. As depicted in Table 6.13, average teacher's salary had a T-statistic of −2.752, which was statistically significant ($p < .05$). These results suggested that a negative relationship exists between achievement test scores of African American males and average teachers' salaries. As the average teacher's salary decreased, the achievement test scores of African American males tended to increase.

African American Females

As noted in Table 6.14, the adjusted R Square for African American females was .08293, which reflected an F value of 2.1800. This statistically significant ($p < .05$) value indicated that a linear relationship existed between achievement test scores and the eleven school characteristics. The adjusted R square value suggested that approximately 8% of the variance in the test scores was related to the selected school characteristics. Statistical results shown in Table 6.15 note that school income level has a T-statistic of 2.793. This value suggested that a statistically significant ($p < .05$) relationship exists between income and test scores of African American females. As the achievement test scores increased for this group, the income level of the school attended increased.

TABLE 6.14 Multiple Regression Statistics for African American Females

Multiple R	.45276
R Squared	.20499
Adjusted Square	.08293
Standard Error	17.36995

Analysis of Variance

	DF	Sum of Squares	Mean Squares
Regression	11	8720.69157	7792.79014
Residual	93	33820.50843	363.66138

F = 2.18002	Significance of F = .0219

TABLE 6.15 Multiple Regression Statistics for African American Females

Variables	Beta	T	Significance of T
Percentage African American students	−.37648	−1.461	.1473
Average teacher salary	−.17114	−1.432	.1554
Age of school building	−.12260	−1.207	.2305
School income	.37602	2.793	.0063
Substitute expenditures	.15699	1.223	.2244
Instructional expenditures	.36901	2.518	.0135
Percentage African American teachers	−1.0003	.691	.4914
Percentage with advanced degrees	−.10966	−.006	.9951
Average class size	−.12389	−.715	.4762
Library books	−.05275	2.834	.0056
Student–Teacher ratio	.56275	−.265	.7917
(Constant)			.5285

Further analysis of the data found that instructional expenditures had a T-value of 2.518. Accordingly, this variable was statistically significant ($p < .05$) in explaining the variance in test scores. The results suggested that as achievement test scores increased for African American females, the income level of the school attended increased. The number of library books per school was also found to be statistically significant ($p < .05$) in explaining the variance in test scores of African American females. As displayed in Table 6.15, the T statistic, 2.834 indicated that as the number of library books in schools attended by African American females increased, the achievement test scores increased. Therefore, a positive relationship exists.

African American Students Bused for Integration

According to results noted in Table 6.16, the Multiple R for bused African American students indicated that a positive relationship existed between the achievement test scores and the eleven selected school characteristics. While the adjusted R square indicated that approximately 10 percent of the variation in test scores was explained linear regression on the school characteristics variables. The F value, 2.015, indicated that there was a statistically significant relationship between the dependent and independent variables.

TABLE 6.16   Multiple Regression Statistics for Bused African American Students

Multiple R	.45275
R Squared	.20499
Adjusted Square	.10330
Standard Error	19.68994

Analysis of Variance

	DF	Sum of Squares	Mean Squares
Regression	11	8596.74670	781.52243
Residual	86	33341.67167	387.69386

F = 2.01582   Significance of F = .0363

TABLE 6.17   Multiple Regression Statistics for Bused African American Students

Variables	Beta	T	Significance of T
Percentage African American Students	−.56002	−1.870	.0648
Average teacher salary	−.08263	−.721	.4728
Age of school building	−.10965	−1.018	.3113
Substitute Expenditures	.09083	.707	.4812
School Income	.44813	2.949	.0041
Instructional Expenditures	.20137	1.396	.1664
Percentage with advanced degrees	−.16482	−.956	.3418
Percentage African American teachers	.11831	.684	.4957
Library books	.20907	1.189	.2375
Average class size	.12290	.593	.5549
Student–Teacher ratio	−.31193	−1.483	.1417
(Constant)		.434	.6652

As noted, 98 African American students rode the bus to schools outside of their neighborhoods during the year of busing mandated for integration. An analysis of data Table 6.17 suggested that the income level of the school to which African Americans were bused was statistically significant ($p < .05$) in explaining the variance in test scores. As shown, the T-statistic for school income level was 2.949. This finding suggested that there is a positive relationship between school income level and achievement test scores of bused African American students. All other variables were found to be insignificant in explaining variance.

Non-Bused African Americans

Table 6.18 indicates that the Multiple R value .37235 suggested a positive relationship between the selected school characteristics and achievement test scores. The adjusted R square for the eleven independent variables was .07864. This finding suggested that approximately 7% of the total variance in test scores for non-bused African American students is explained by selected school characteristics. The F-value of 2.3211 was found to be statistically significant ($p < .05$). These findings suggested that a linear relationship exists between the dependent and independent variables. It has been previously noted that 105 female African American students attended schools in their neighborhoods during the year of mandated busing and attended the same school after the elimination of the policy. Test results indicated that the selected independent variables were not statistically significant in explaining the variance in achievement test scores (Table 6.19).

Chapter 1 African Americans

Findings in Table 6.20 indicated that the Multiple R suggested a positive relationship between achievement test scores and the eleven school characteristics. The adjusted square of .07491 indicated that approximately 7% of the variation in the test scores was explained by linear regression on the school characteristics. The F value of 2.15574 was statistically significant ($p < .05$). The results suggested that the linear relationship between the test scores and selected school characteristics was statistically significant for African America Chapter 1 participants.

Previous statistical data indicated that 45 African Americans in this sample participated in Chapter 1 during the resegregated school year. Data analysis suggested that a linear relationship existed. These results imply that as the school income level increased, the achievement test scores of Chapter 1 African American students increased. Further analysis indicated

TABLE 6.18   Multiple Regression Statistics for Non-Bused African American Students

Multiple R	.37235
R Squared	.13864
Adjusted Square	.07864
Standard Error	17.22529

Analysis of Variance

	DF	Sum of Squares	Mean Squares
Regression	11	7545.75784	685.97799
Residual	158	46880.29510	296.71030

F = 2.31194   Significance of F = .0118

TABLE 6.19   Multiple Regression Statistics for Non-Bused African American Students

Variables	Beta	T	Significance of T
Percentage African American students	.51885	.520	.6040
Percentage African American teachers	.46464	1.546	.1254
Age of school building	.09374	.552	.5825
School income	−.27645	−.455	.6504
Substitute expenditures	−.09926	−.377	.7073
Average class size	−.25426	−1.420	.1590
Percentage with advanced degrees	.48315	1.805	.0743
Instructional expenditures	.28062	1.016	.3124
Student–Teacher ratio	.10982	.400	.6901
Average teacher salary	−.39304	−.839	.4037
Library books	−.66703	−.590	.5565
(Constant)		1.178	.2417

that the school expenditures had a T-statistic of 2.093, which was statistically significant ($p < .05$). As the amount of money spent on instructional expenditures increased, the achievement test scores of African American students increased. Additionally, as the number of library books increased, achievement test scores increased (Table 6.21).

TABLE 6.20 Multiple Regression Statistics for Chapter 1 African American Students

	Multiple R	.37380
	R Squared	.13972
	Adjusted Square	.07491
	Standard Error	17.75529

Analysis of Variance

	DF	Sum of Squares	Mean Squares
Regression	11	7475.58716	679.59883
Residual	146	46026.56474	315.25044
F = 2.31194		Significance of F = .0118	

TABLE 6.21 Multiple Regression Statistics for Chapter 1 African American Students

Variables	Beta	T	Significance of T
Percentage African American students	−.88945	−2.034	.0501
Average teacher salary	−.07363	−.409	.6854
Age of school building	.15207	.866	.3927
Substitute expenditures	.21280	1.036	.3076
School income	.84931	3.056	.0044
Instructional expenditures	.67939	2.093	.0441
Percentage African American teachers	−.25332	−1.549	.2567
Percentage with advanced degrees	.07996	.297	.7687
Average class size	.05143	.181	.8576
Student–Teacher ratio	−.34174	−.961	.3434
Library books	1.10643	2.754	.0095
(Constant)		−.216	.8302

Non-Chapter 1 African Americans

Analysis of results also indicated (Table 6.22) that 148 African Americans did not participate in the Chapter 1 program during the resegregation year. The T- statistic, −2.620 suggested that a negative statistically significant re-

TABLE 6.22 Selected Multiple Regression Statistics for Non-Chapter 1 African American Students

Variables	Beta	T	Significance of T
Percentage African American students	–.60667	–2.620	.0097
Average teacher salary	–.37950	–3.181	.0018
Age of school building	–.11987	–1.501	.1356
Substitute expenditures	–.09877	–.803	.4230
School income	.31627	–2.829	.0053
Instructional expenditures	.08229	.696	.4872
Percentage with advanced degrees	.10654	.799	.4258
Percentage African American teachers	.28363	1.987	.0488
Library books	.07325	.470	.6389
Student–Teacher ratio	–.14481	–.938	.3498
Average class size	–.12534	–.777	.4386
(Constant)		2.393	.0180

lationship between African American student percentage and the achievement test scores of non-Chapter 1 African American students. As the percent of non-Chapter 1 African American students in a school increased, the achievement test scores of African American students tended to decrease.

The average teachers' salary also appeared to account for variance in test scores of non-Chapter 1 African Americans. Average teachers' salary had a T-value of –3181. This value indicated a statistically significant ($p < .05$) negative relationship between test scores and average teachers' salary. Results suggested that as these salaries increased in a given school, the achievement test scores of African American non-Chapter 1 African American students decreased. Additional data analysis suggests that the T-value for school income level was also significant. As the income level of a school increased, the achievement test scores on non-Chapter 1 students increased.

Findings also show that the percentage of African American teachers in a school attended by African American Chapter 1 students was positively related to the achievement test scores. The T-statistic, 1.987 was statistically significant ($p < .05$). As the percentage of African American Teachers increased, the achievement test scores for non-Chapter 1 African American students increased.

Summary

The findings of this study suggested that significant differences existed between the achievement test scores of African American fourth grade African American students during the integration of the schools and after the return to neighborhood schools. Further analysis of the data indicated that the eleven selected school characteristics accounted for 8% of the variance in test scores for all African American students; 9% for African American males; 11% for African American females; 10% for all bused Americans; 5% for non-bused African Americans; 7% for Chapter 1 African Americans, and 7% for non-Chapter 1 African Americans.

European American Students, School Characteristics and the Achievement Gap

As shown in Table 6.23, 228 European American fourth grade students were included in this sample. The mean score for this group during the year of busing was 68.48; however, the mean declined to 65.40 after the return to neighborhood schools. The mean difference was statistically significant ($p < .05$). The results suggested that European American students performed better on achievement tests during the existence of the desegregation policy.

The findings in Table 6.24 indicated that 129 members of the sample were European American males. The mean scores for this group were 66.84 during the existence of the policy.

TABLE 6.23   T-Test Results: Achievement Gap between African American and European American Students During Desegregation for Desegregated European American Students

Grade	Number of cases	Mean	Standard Deviation	Standard Error
African Americans	203	47.15	23.15	1.61
European Americans	228	65.40	23.42	1.54
Achievement Gap 18.25				

TABLE 6.24   Busing and Post-Busing Achievement Gaps for European American Males

Grade	Number of cases	Mean	*t* value	df	2-tail
3 Bused	129	66.84	2.93	128	.004
4 Non-bused	129	62.21			

This mean declined to 62.21 after the return to neighborhood schools. The results of the T-test statistics suggested that the decline in scores was statistically significant ($p < .05$). European American males performed better on achievement tests during the mandated busing year. Table 6.25 indicated that the T-test statistic yielded different results for the 99 European American females included in this sample. The mean score during the year of mandated busing was 70.61. After the elimination of the policy, the mean declined to 69.52. Unlike their male counterparts, this decrease in the mean was statistically insignificant. The results suggest that the achievement test scores of European American females did not change significantly. Based upon these findings, multiple regression statistical models were selected for further analysis.

In an effort to identify the variables that may explain the decline in achievement test scores for European American fourth grade students, the same eleven school characteristics were selected as independent variables tested (Table 6.26) The differences between school characteristics

TABLE 6.25 Busing and Post-Busing Achievement Gaps for European American Females

Grade		Number of cases	Mean	*t* value	df	2-tail
3	Bused	99	70.61	.77	98	.444
4	Non-bused	99	69.52			

TABLE 6.26 Multiple Regression Statistics for All NPS European American Students

Variables	Beta	T	Significance of T
Percentage African American students	–.07360	–.689	.4913
Library books	.09085	1.201	.2312
Substitute expenditures	–.05817	–.496	.6207
Age of school building	–.05695	–.772	.4408
Percentage with advanced degrees	–.14305	–.905	.3663
School income	.07263	.856	.3929
Instructional expenditures	.01793	.202	.8399
Average class size	.03027	.243	.8079
Percentage African American teachers	—	.051	.9597
Student–Teacher ratio	.09012	.860	.3909
Average teacher salary	–.28750	–1.772	.0778
(Constant)		1.374	.1710

during mandated busing for desegregation and after its elimination were computed and analyzed. The Multiple R square indicated a positive relationship between test scores and selected school characteristics. The adjusted R square indicated that approximately 12% of the variance in test scores of all European American students and the eleven school characteristics was shown to be significant at $(p < .05)$. Further analysis of the data suggested that no one-school characteristic was statistically significant in explaining total variance in test scores.

European American Males

Data analysis indicated a Multiple R value of .4187, which suggested the existence of a positive relationship between the dependent and independent variables for European American males. The adjusted R square for the eleven school characteristics was .0977 with an F value of 2.261. These values suggested that approximately 10 percent of the variance in the achievement test scores for European American males may be accounted for by the eleven school characteristics. The F value suggested that this 10% variance was statistically significant. Additional analyses of the data indicated that no one-school characteristic was significant in explaining the variance in test scores for European American males (Table 6.27).

TABLE 6.27   Multiple Regression Statistics for European American Males

Variables	Beta	T	Significance of T
Percentage African American students	−.04341	−.284	.7765
Library books	.11561	1.142	.2560
Substitute expenditures	−.11607	−.670	.5040
Age of school building	−.15804	1.630	.1058
Average teacher salary	−.26786	−.957	.3408
School income	−.01612	.123	.9025
Instructional expenditures	.03506	.306	.7601
Student–Teacher ratio	.15095	1.067	.2883
Average class size	−.03452	−.142	.8871
Percentage African American teachers	.02957	.163	.8707
Percentage with advanced degrees	−.13186	−.479	.6330
(Constant)		.645	.5203

European American Females

The statistical results support similar findings for European American males and European American females. The statistical test results yielded an adjusted R square of .170 for European American females. This finding suggested that 17% of the total variance in test scores can be attributed to the eleven selected school characteristics. The R square indicated a significant relationship between test scores and school characteristics. Further analysis of the T value (Table 6.28) suggested that no one-school characteristic was significant in explaining the total variance in test scores for European American females.

Bused European American Students

During the year of mandated busing for desegregation, the scores of bused Europe segregation, 75 European American students rode the bus to schools outside their neighborhoods. The Multiple R value suggested a positive relationship between the test scores of bused European American students and school characteristics. However, the adjusted R square has a negative value of –.0813. These statistics suggested that approximately 8% of the variance in test scores was attributed to school characteristics. Further analysis of the data, as depicted in Table 6.29, indicated that no one-school characteristic could explain the variance in test scores for this group.

TABLE 6.28 Multiple Regression Statistics for NPS European American Females

Variables	Beta	T	Significance of T
Percentage African American students	–.20146	–1.096	.2761
Substitute expenditures	.14649	.790	.4314
Library books	.10067	.622	.5358
School income	.18502	1.471	.1450
Age of school building	.06965	.582	.5619
Percentage with advanced degrees	–.27198	–1.337	.1846
Percentage African American teachers	–.13742	–.844	.4009
Average class size	.06629	.415	.6791
Instructional expenditures	.07569	.507	.6135
Student–Teacher ratio	–.05328	–.289	.7729
Average teacher salary	–.28124	–1.260	.2110
(Constant)		1.003	.3136

TABLE 6.29   Multiple Regression Statistics for NPS European American Bused Students

Variables	Beta	T	Significance of T
Percentage African American students	.10976	.545	.5877
Substitute expenditures	.12277	.558	.5791
Average teacher salary	.11581	.583	.5617
Library books	.10497	.745	.4590
School income	.08673	.378	.7060
Student–Teacher ratio	.05288	.295	.7690
Age of school building	−.05713	−.319	.7507
Instructional expenditures	.02647	.148	.8828
Percentage African American teachers	−.17100	−.958	.3417
Average class size	.21363	.881	.3818
Percentage with advanced degrees	−.24256	−.929	.3565
(Constant)		.296	.7685

Non-bused European American Students

During the existence of the policy of mandated busing, 153 European American students attended schools in their neighborhood. The adjusted R Square for non-bused European American students was .18373, which represented a F value of 4.80150. This statistically significant value indicated that a linear relationship exists between achievement test scores and the eleven selected school characteristics. The adjusted R square indicated that approximately 18% of the variance was related to school characteristics. As shown in Table 6.30, further examination of data results indicated a negative relationship between test scores and student percentage African American. The T value of −2.169 was found to be significant. As the percentage of African American students in a given school decreased, the achievement test scores of European American non-bused students increased. The T statistic of −2.262 indicated that a negative relationship between class size and achievement test scores of non-bused European American students. As the average class size of a given school decreased, the achievement test scores of this group increased. The amount of money spent for substitute teachers was negatively related inversely proportional to the achievement test scores of non-bused European American students. Substitute teacher expenditures had a T value of −2.317, which suggested that as the number of substitute teachers utilized for given schools increased, the achievement test scores for non-bused European American students decreased. The av-

TABLE 6.30 Multiple Regression Statistics for European American Non-Bused Students

Variables	Beta	T	Significance of T
Percentage African American students	−2.01604	−2.169	.0317
Percentage African American teachers	1.32723	2.274	.0245
School income	.12418	1.015	.3119
Library books	−.46027	−1.757	.0811
Age of school building	.40825	1.619	.1076
Average class size	−.89805	−2.262	.0252
Substitute expenditures	−1.68088	−2.317	.0219
Instructional expenditures	−.81832	−1.765	.0797
Average teacher salary	−2.77775	−2.557	.0116
(Constant)		1.697	.0917

Variables not in equation:
    Student–Teacher ratio
    Percentage with advanced degrees

erage teachers' salary was also statistically significant in explaining the variance in test scores of non-bused European American students. The negative T-value, −2.557 indicated that as the average teacher's salary increased, achievement test scores decreased.

Chapter 1 European American Students

A multiple R .85482 indicated a strong linear relationship between the test scores of European American Chapter 1 students and school characteristics. However, the small sample size may contribute to an inflated R statistic. Twenty-six students were enrolled in the Chapter 1 program. The adjusted R square for this group was .51913 with an F value of 3.4554, which was significant. The eleven school characteristics appeared to explain 52% of the variance in test scores for European American Chapter 1 students. As noted, the T value of each independent variable was statistically insignificant.

Table 6.31 indicates that a positive relationship existed between achievement test scores and the eleven characteristics for non-Chapter 1 European American students. The adjusted R square of .12440 indicated that approximately 12 % of the variation in the test scores was explained by linear regression on the school characteristics. The F value of 3.5961 indicated that these results were significant in explaining variance in test scores.

TABLE 6.31 Multiple Regression Statistics for European American Chapter 1 Students

Variables	Beta	T	Significance of T
Percentage African American students	−2.25408	−2.080	.0564
Percentage with advanced degrees	4.08939	1.365	.1939
Library books	−.36148	−.911	.3777
Substitute expenditures	−.77954	−.809	.4318
Average teacher salary	−2.99314	−1.631	.1251
Instructional expenditures	.78530	1.301	.2143
Percentage African American teachers	.69680	1.112	.2851
Age of school building	−.07583	−.179	.8607
Student–Teacher ratio	−.21809	−.458	.6541
Average class size	−2.47164	−1.919	.0756
School income	2.07857	1.556	.1421
(Constant)		1.481	.1608

Non-Chapter 1 European American Students

The Multiple Regression R suggested that a positive relationship existed between achievement test scores and the eleven school characteristics. The adjusted square of .12440 indicated that approximately 12% of the variation in the test score could be explained by a linear relationship. Further data analysis (Table 6.32), The F value of 3.59618 indicated that these results were statistically significant ($p < .05$) in explaining this linear relationship. Further analysis of data indicated that no one-school characteristics was statistically significant in explaining the variance in test scores. In sum, the T statistics were not statistically significant.

Summary: European American Students

The findings of this research study suggested that significant differences exited between the achievement test scores of European American fourth grade students during mandated busing for desegregation and their achievement test scores after the elimination of the policy.

Further analysis suggested that the eleven selected school characteristics explained a small percentage of the variance in test scores. The school characteristics accounted for 12% of the variance in test scores for all European American students, 10% for European American males, 17% for Europe American females, 8% for all bused European American students, 18% for non-bused European Americans, and 52% for Chapter 1 European Ameri-

TABLE 6.32   Multiple Regression Statistics for European American Non-Chapter 1 Students

Variables	Beta	T	Significance of T
Percentage African American students	−.02400	−.269	.7885
Substitute expenditures	−.14239	−1.092	.2763
Library books	.10983	1.415	.1587
Age of school building	.07108	−.889	.3752
School income	.01822	−.207	.8365
Instructional expenditures	−.02400	−.255	.7987
Average teacher salary	−.28355	−1.626	.1057
Average class size	.10508	.834	.4055
Student–Teacher ratio	.10389	.967	.3356
Percentage African American teachers	.07597	.631	.5285
Percentage with advanced degrees	.18935	−1.160	.2477
(Constant)		1.437	.1524

TABLE 6.33   T-Test Results: Achievement Gap between African American and European American Students During Desegregation for Desegregated European American Students

Grade	Number of cases	Mean	Standard Deviation	Standard Error
African Americans	203	52.57	18.428	1.287
European Americans	228	68.48	18.289	

Achievement Gap   15.91

cans and 12% for non-bused European Americans. However, the variance in test scores of European American females was found to be statistically insignificant. Their busing/post-busing achievement test scores were not affected by the changes in school characteristics.

As shown is Table 6.33, the mean score for African Americans during mandated busing was 52.57 and 68.48 for European Americans. This represented a difference of 15.91. The mean score for African Americans after the elimination of mandated busing was 47.15 and 65.38 for European Americans. This represented a gap of 18.22. The achievement gap between African Americans and European Americans, increased by 2.31 points after the elimination of mandated busing.

This study indicated that the achievement gap increased between African Americans and European Americans after the elimination of mandated busing for integration. The difference between selected school characteristics did not appear to be statistically significant in explaining the variance in test scores for African.

Summary of Findings

The sample for this study was randomly selected from eleven Norfolk Public Elementary schools. Ninety-eight African American males were included in this study, 129 European American males; 105 African American females; and 99 European American females. The total sample size was 431. The T-test statistical procedure was performed to determine if statistically significant differences existed between the busing/post-busing score of fourth-grade students. Additionally, multiple linear regression analysis was utilized to examine variables that may have influenced variance in test scores. Analyses of data generated by this study indicated that the elimination of the policy of mandated busing for integration had a significant negative effect on the overall achievement scores of African American and European American fourth-grade students in the Norfolk Public Schools District. The selected school characteristics explained only small percentage of the variance in test scores.

Further investigation revealed that the changes in school characteristics resulting from the policy of mandated busing accounted for approximately 8% of the decline in test scores of all African American students. The school's income level, the percentage of African American students in a given school, and average teachers' salary were statistically significant in explaining the variance in test scores of all African American students. Results also indicated that as the percentage of African American students in a given school increased, the achievement test scores of African American students decreased. This same negative relationship was observed in the average teacher's salary level of a given school. Unlike the previous two variables, school income level was positively related to the achievement test scores of African American students. As the average income level of a school increased, the achievement test scores of African Americans increased.

The findings for African American males suggested that only 9% of the variance in test scores can be attributed to selected school characteristics. However, this 9% variance was not statistically significant in explaining the variance. Most of the variance in test scores of African American males was accounted for by the percentage of African American teachers in a school, by the school income level, and by average teachers' salary.

The results of this investigation suggested that as the percentage of African American teachers in a given school increased, the achievement test scores of African American males increased. The income level of a given school was found to be positively related to the achievement test scores of African American males. Findings suggested that as average teacher's salary increased, achievement test scores increased for African American males decreased.

Somewhat different findings were noted with African American females. Approximately 11% of the variance in their test scores was attributed to the eleven selected school characteristics. The statistical results indicated that as the amount of money spent on instructional materials increased, the achievement test scores of African American females increased. A positive relationship was found with the number of library books. As the number of library books in a school increased, achievement test scores tended to increase. The relationship between school income level and achievement test scores was found to be the same for both African American males and females.

The selected school characteristics were found to account for approximately 10% of the variance in the test scores of all bused African American students. The majority of this variance was attributed to the school income level. Again, as the school income level increased, the achievement test scores for bused African American students increased. The findings for non-bused African Americans differed. The selected school characteristics accounted for about 5% of the variance in test scores. However, this 5% was found to be insignificant. The findings suggested that no one-school characteristic was significant in explaining the variance in test scores of non-bused African American students.

AFRICAN AMERICAN STUDENTS

The results of this study also showed that 14% of the variance in achievement test scores of Chapter 1 African American students may be attributed to the selected school characteristics. Statistical results suggested that as the school income level increased the achievement test scores of Chapter 1 females increased. The same finding was noted with instructional expenditures. As the amount of money spent for instructional materials increased, the achievement test scores of African American Chapter 1 students increased. Approximately 7% of the variance in the test scores was accounted for by the selected school characteristics. This variance was attributed to the percentage of African American students in a school, to school income level and to average teacher's salary. Accordingly, as the percentage of African American students in a school increased, the achievement test scores of African American non-chapter 1 students decreased.

This same negative relationship was found with teacher's salaries. However, findings indicated that as the percentage of African American teachers in a given school increased, the achievement test scores of African American non-Chapter 1 students increased.

Further analysis of data generated by this study found that the elimination of the policy of mandated busing for integration had a significant negative effect on the overall achievement test scores of European American students. The selected schools explained only a small percentage of the variance in test scores.

EUROPEAN AMERICAN STUDENTS

The results of this study indicated that approximately 12% of the variance in test scores of European American students may be explained by changes in school characteristics. However, it was concluded that no one selected school characteristic was significant in explaining the variance in test scores. Similar findings were noted for European American males and females.

The selected school characteristics may explain approximately 10 and 17% of the variance in test scores of European males and females respectively. However, no one-school characteristic was significant. Results suggested that 8% of the variance in test scores was attributed to school characteristics. However, no significant relationship existed between achievement test scores and school characteristics for bused European American students. This was not the case for non-bused European American students. Data indicated that 18% of the variance may be explained by the percentage of African American students in a given school, by the percentage of African American teachers, substitute teacher expenditures, or by average teacher's salary. These results found that as the percentage of African American students in a school increased, the achievement test scores of non-bused European American students tended to decrease. However, a positive relationship was observed with the percentage of African American teachers in a school. As the percentage of African American teachers in a school increased, the achievement scores on non-bused European American students increased.

Negative relationships were noted with teachers' salary level and substitute expenditures. Accordingly, as the average teacher's salary increased, the achievement test scores of non-bused European American students tended to decrease.

Analysis of data also revealed that as the amount of money spent on substitute teachers increased, the achievement test scores for non-bused students decreased. The number of European American Chapter 1 students was too small to compute reliable measures for reliable measurement; therefore, those findings are not accurate. Findings indicated that

12% of the variance in test scores may be attributed to school characteristics. However, no one-school characteristic was significant. An analysis of data also indicated that a statistically significant difference existed between the achievement test scores of African American and European American students. The mean achievement test score was significantly higher for European American students than their African American counterparts. The achievement gap between the two groups increased after the elimination of mandated busing for integration and the return to segregated schooling. Findings indicated that African American and European American fourth-grade students in the Norfolk Public Schools district performed significantly better on achievement tests during the year of mandated busing. The findings of this study suggested that the elimination of the policy of mandated busing and the return to a segregated system resulted in changes in school characteristics that increased the achievement gap between African American and European American students. The achievement test scores of African American students declined more than did the scores of European American students. The selected school characteristics explained only 10% of the decline in test scores for African American students. No conclusive evidence can be cited by this study in explaining the decline in test scores for African American students. However, the scores of African American males declined more than African American females. Historically, African American females have performed better on achievement tests than their African American male counterparts. The results from this study support this. Although the achievement test scores of European American students experienced a decline after the elimination of the policy of mandated busing, the scores of European American female students appeared to be less affected by changes in school characteristics that resulted from the elimination of mandated busing than their European American male counterparts. The selected school characteristics explained 12% of the variance in test scores of European American students. No conclusive evidence was found in this study to explain the variance in test scores for European American students.

Finally, the evidence indicated that the achievement gap between European American and African American students increased after the schools resegregated. As shown in Table. 6.34, none of the school characteristics appeared to correlate with achievement test scores of European American students. However, this was not the case for African American students. The racial composition of the school was a correlate for all African American students as a group; however, it was not evident for African American females. The income level (socioeconomic level of the community) was also a correlate for both male and female African American students. Instructional expenditures and the number of library book in the school were additional correlates for African American females. Average teacher salary was also a correlate for African American males.

When one investigates the correlates further, it becomes apparent that the percentage of African American students attending a given school is a correlate for all students (Table 6.35). In other words, as the percentage of African American students increases, achievement declines. Again, school

TABLE 6.34   Correlates: School Characteristics and Achievement Gap Test Scores

Correlates	African Americans			European Americans		
	All	Males	Females	All	Males	Females
School % African American	Yes	Yes				
School income level	Yes	Yes	Yes			
Substitute expenditures						
Instructional expenditures			Yes			
Average teacher salary	Yes	Yes				
% advanced degree						
Number of library books			Yes			
Average class size						
% African American teachers		Yes				
Student–Teacher ratio						
Age of school building						

TABLE: 6.35   Correlates: School Characteristics and Achievement Gap Test Scores

Correlates	All males	All females	All students
School % African American			Yes
School income level	Yes	Yes	Yes
Substitute expenditures			
Instructional expenditures			
Average teacher salary	Yes	Yes	Yes
% advanced degree			
Number of library books		Yes	
Average class size			
% African American teachers			
Student–Teacher ratio			
Age of school building	Yes		

income level and average teacher salary were shown to be correlates for all male and female students in this sample. The number of library books was also a correlate for all females, but not the male students.

For those students who were bused for desegregation, school income level was a correlate for All African Americans (Table 6.36), bused females and all bused students. It is also interesting to note that substitute

TABLE 6.36 Correlates: School Characteristics and Achievement Gap Test Scores for Desegregated Students

Correlates	African Americans	All European Americans	Bused Students		
			Males	Females	All
School % African American					
School income level	Yes			Yes	Yes
Substitute expenditures				Yes	
Instructional expenditures					
Average teacher salary					
% advanced degree					
Number of library books					
Average class size					
% African American teachers				Yes	
Student–Teacher ratio					
Age of school building					

TABLE 6.37 Correlates: School Characteristics and Achievement Gap Test Scores for Resegregated Students

Correlates	Non-Bused African Americans	Non-Bused European Americans	Non-Bused Students		
			Males	Females	All
School % African American		Yes			
School income level					
Substitute expenditures		Yes			
Instructional expenditures					
Average teacher salary				Yes	Yes
% advanced degree					
Number of library books					
Average class size		Yes		Yes	Yes
% African American teachers		Yes			
Student–Teacher ratio					
Age of school building					

expenditures and the percentage of African American teachers in a given school appeared as correlates. However, for those students attending re-segregated schools the correlates were a bit different (Table 6.37). The percentage of African American students was a correlate for non-bused (resegregated) European American females. Substitute expenditures, average class size, and the percentage of African American teachers in a given school are also correlates for non-bused (resegregated) European American females. Average teacher salary and class size were correlates for all resegregated females.

CHAPTER 7

THE ACHIEVEMENT GAP IN THE RESEGREGATED NORFOLK CITY PUBLIC SCHOOLS

There is a brilliant child locked inside every student.
—Marva Collins, 2006

It has become apparent to many that separate can never be equal. Many have made the long journey from Topeka to Seattle and now realize that public school districts may have come full circle in terms of the struggle for equality. The reality is that in the search for equal opportunity, many have struggled through four main historical stages: the 1896 battle equality when Plessy battled segregation; the 1930s battle for equality in our colleges and universities; the 1954 *Brown* decision in which the K–12 challenge to separatism in the nation's public schools, and the 2007 Seattle ruling, which reversed *Brown*. Although this is 2009 and not 1954, many of the issues relevant to the achievement gap between African American and European American students continue to pervade. A review of the research conducted by scholars (Chapter 4) has long supported this contention. Equity appears to be a central theme in the Norfolk City Public School District; therefore, this chapter will review the status of the achievement gap in the district's public schools.

Narrowing the Achievement Gap in a (Re)Segregated Urban School District, pages 113–126
Copyright © 2009 by Information Age Publishing

THE DISTRICT'S ACHIEVEMENT GAP IN 2008

Analysis of 2008 data indicated that 59% of African American students passed the eighth-grade mathematics Standards of Learning (SOL) tests as compared to 75% Hispanic, and 81% European American students. Females outperformed their male counterpart, 69% and 62% respectively.

The district's disadvantaged group performed similarly to males with a pass rate of 60%. Findings also indicated that 60% of English language learners passed the mathematics test. Grade eight reading results indicated the following pass rates: 61% African Americans; 67% Hispanics; 84% European Americans; 70% females; 67% males; 60% disadvantaged learners; and 56% English Language Learners. European American students and females outperformed all other subgroups in reading.

As presented in Figure 7.1, fourth-grade SOL mathematics pass rates indicated that the gap between Hispanics and European Americans is 4 percentage points, whereas the gap between African American and European American students is 14 points. Additionally, females outperformed males; there was a 3-percentage point gap between the two groups. The pass rate for the disadvantage and African American students was the same at 75%. Given the number of disadvantaged African American students in the dis-

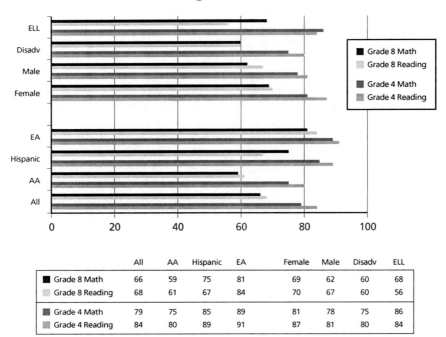

	All	AA	Hispanic	EA	Female	Male	Disadv	ELL
■ Grade 8 Math	66	59	75	81	69	62	60	68
▨ Grade 8 Reading	68	61	67	84	70	67	60	56
▨ Grade 4 Math	79	75	85	89	81	78	75	86
▨ Grade 4 Reading	84	80	89	91	87	81	80	84

Figure 7.1   NPS SOL percentage pass by subgroups: Reading and mathematics, 2008.

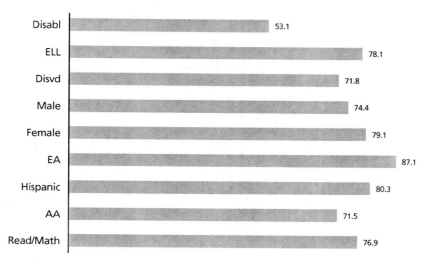

Figure 7.2   NPS 2008 SOL reading and mathematics proficiency subgroup.

trict, this is not a surprise. The fourth-grade reading pass rates were: 80% African Americans; 89%, Hispanics; 91% European Americans; 87% females; 81% males; 80% disadvantaged; and 84% English Language Learners. Again, with the exception of the disadvantaged, all subgroups outperformed African American students in reading.

An additional review of data indicated that 87% of the district's European Americans passed both science and mathematics SOL tests. (Figure 7.2) Gaps among other subgroups are evident in terms of the following pass rates: African Americans 71.5%; Hispanics, 80.3%; females, 79.1; males, 74.4%; 71.8% disadvantaged; English Language Learners and disabled students, 53.1%. Only the disabled subgroup performed lower than African American students.

THE DISTRICT'S ACHIEVEMENT GAP BY SUB GROUPS

The Norfolk school districts stratifies and reports achievement gap data utilizing two groupings: *racial ethnic gaps*, used to compare academic performance of African American, Hispanic, and European American students; and *income gaps* used to compare the performance of low income students to non-low-income students.

It must also be noted that achievement gaps are represented by negative numbers in the district data reports, and the closing of gaps is represented by positive numbers. The district measures the achievement gap in three different ways: (a) internal districts gaps, (b) internal district vs. internal state gap, and (c) external gap district disadvantaged vs. state disadvantaged. Additionally, the following key terms are utilized in interpreting the data:

- *Income Gaps*: A comparison of the performance of low-income students with non-low-income students.
- *Racial/Ethnic Gaps*: A comparison of the performance of African American and Hispanic students with European American students.

Additionally, the district analyzes the achievement gap in terms of:

- *Internal District Gap*: The gap in performance between the districts.
- *Internal District vs. Internal State Gap*: The district's internal gap minus the state's internal gap.
- *External Gap*: The gap in performance between the districts. This measure is used to compare the performance of the districts disadvantaged group with that of the state's disadvantaged groups. (Broad Foundation, 2008, pp. 25–29)

The Internal District Gap in Reading

Elementary School Reading Gaps

The internal achievement gap (Table 7.1) between African and American and European American students in reading declined from 17 percentage points in 2004, to 11 in 2007. The achievement gap increased from –10 in 2006, to –1 in 2007. This represented a 1% increase in the gap. Although these findings suggest that African American students in the district are closing the achievement gap in reading, the racial gap still exits. A closer examination of the data indicates that the gap between low-income and non-low-income students also declined between 2004 and 2007. Low-income students in the districts had a pass rate of 13 percentage points less (–13) than their non-low-income counterparts in 2004. In 2006 and 2007, the income gap was unchanged at –6.

Middle School Reading Gap

The internal district gap in reading between middle-school African American and European American students was –24 in 2004 (Table 6.4). The gap declined to –18 in 2005 and remained at that hat level the following year. However, by 2007 this gap had decreased to –17. The –18 in 2006, suggested that there was little change in the gap between these two groups in 2007 (Table 7.2). Similar findings became apparent in analyzing the internal district gap when comparing low-income and non-low-income groups. There was a 16-percentage point pass rate gap in 2004 (–16) and

TABLE 7.1   Norfolk Elementary Reading Achievement Gaps 2004–2007

Elementary	2004	2005	2006	2007	2006–07 Change	Gap Closure Type
Internal District Gap						
African American/European American	−17	−9	−10	−11	−1	—
Hispanic/European American	*	*	*	*	*	*
Low Income/Non-Low Income	−13	−9	−9	−11	−2	—
Internal District vs. Internal state Gap						
African American/European American	2	6	4	2	−2	—
Hispanic/European American	*	*	*	*	*	*
Low Income/Non-Low Income	−16	−11	−11	−10	1	—
External Gap District Disadvantaged vs. State Disadvantaged						
African American/European American	−16	−11	−10	−10	0	—
Hispanic/European American	*	*	*	*	*	*
Low Income/Non-Low Income						2

Source: The Eli and Edythe Broad Foundation: Analysis of State Test Data (2008)
Notes:
  — indicates data not available
  * indicates calculation was not performed
  1 Both Advantaged and disadvantaged groups are increasing. The gap is closing
    because the disadvantaged group proficiencies are increasing at a faster rate than their
    disadvantaged counterparts.
  2 The gap is closing; however, proficiency for the advantaged group did not change or has
    declined.

a −16 gap in 2007. In essence, the income gap remained constant from 2004–2007. These findings indicate that non-low-income students continue to have a higher pass rate on given tests than their low-income counterparts and that the income gap did not narrow.

High School Reading Gap

The internal district gap indicated that the reading proficiency achievement gap between African American and European American high-school students narrowed between 2004 and 2007. In 2004, there was a 14-percentage point gap (−14) between the two groups. The gap increased to −16 in 2005 and declined significantly to −9 in 2006 and −5 in 2007. This represented a 4-percentage point narrowing of the achievement gap between the two groups in reading between 2006 and 2007. The gap between low-income and non-low-income was −6 in 2004. The gap narrowed in 2006 to −2 and increased to −5 in 2007. The gap change between 2006 and 2007 was −3, which

TABLE 7.2   Norfolk Middle School Reading Achievement Gaps 2004–2007

Middle	2004	2005	2006	2007	2006–07 Change	Gap Closure Type
Internal District Gap						
African American/European American	–24	–18	–18	–17	0	—
Hispanic/European American	*	*	*	*	*	*
Low Income/Non-Low Income	–16	–14	–16	–16	0	—
Internal District vs. Internal state Gap						
African American/European American	0	2	2	0	–2	—
Hispanic/European American	*	*	*	*	*	*
External Gap District Disadvantaged vs. State Disadvantaged						
African American/European American	–19	–19	–20	–19	1	1
Hispanic/European American	*	*	*	*	*	*
Low Income/Non-Low Income	–17	–18	–20	–20	1	1

Source: The Eli and Edythe Broad Foundation: Analysis of State Test Data (2008)
Notes:
— indicates data not available
* indicates calculation was not performed
1 Both Advantaged and disadvantaged groups are increasing. The gap is closing because the disadvantaged group proficiencies are increasing at a faster rate than their disadvantaged counterparts.
2 The gap is closing; however, proficiency for the advantaged group did not change or has declined.

indicated an increase in the income gap between the two groups. As was the case at the middle-school level, the income gap did not narrow (Table 7.3).

Internal District Versus Internal State Gap in Reading

Elementary School Reading Gap

As shown in the previous tables, the internal district/internal state gap indicated that African American students in the school district of Norfolk are doing better than the state in narrowing the reading achievement gap between their European American peers.. In 2004, the gap was 2 points, suggesting that the district's African's American students are performing 2 percentage points above the state's African American students in narrowing the racial achievement gap. The district also did better than the state in 2005, 6 percentage points; 2006, 4 percentage points. However,

TABLE 7.3   Norfolk High School Reading Achievement Gaps 2004–2007

High	2004	2005	2006	2007	2006–07 Change	Gap Closure Type
Internal District Gap						
African American/European American	–14	–16	–9	–5	8	1
Hispanic/European American	*	*	*	*	*	*
Low Income/Non-Low Income	–6	*	–2	–5	3	1
Internal District vs. Internal state Gap						
African American/European American	–1	–2	2	3	4	1
Hispanic/European American	*	*	*	*	*	*
Low Income/Non-Low Income	5	*	8	4	1	1
External Gap District Disadvantaged vs. State Disadvantaged						
African American/European American	–12	–15	–6	–4	9	1
Hispanic/European American	*	*	*	*	*	*
Low Income/Non-Low Income	–9	*	–2	–6	5	1

Source: The Eli and Edythe Broad Foundation: Analysis of State Test Data (2008)
Notes:
— indicates data not available
* indicates calculation was not performed
1 Both Advantaged and disadvantaged groups are increasing. The gap is closing because the disadvantaged group proficiencies are increasing at a faster rate than their disadvantaged counterparts.
2 The gap is closing; however, proficiency for the advantaged group did not change or has declined.

by 2007, the district only outperformed the state by 2 percentage points. This represented a decrease (–2) in performance. Low-income students in the Norfolk school district are also outperforming the state in narrowing the reading achievement gap. In 2004, the district performed 6 percentage points above their non-low-income elementary school counterparts. In 2005, there was an 8 percentage point difference; 8 percentage points in 2005; 5 percentage points in 2006 and 4 percentage points in 2007. The district continued to perform better in narrowing the income gap when compared to the state.

Middle School Reading Gap

As was the case at the elementary level, the district's middle schools also outperformed the state in narrowing the reading achievement gap between African American and European American students. In 2004, the state and district scores did not differ; however, in 2005 and 2006, African American students performed 2 percentage points above the state's African American students in narrowing the achievement gap in reading. There were no differences in the between the two groups in 2007, and this reflected the district's inability to narrow the gap more during this year. The district performed better than the state in narrowing the income gap between low-income and non-low-income students. In 2004, the low-income students scored 9 percentage points higher than their non-low-income counterparts on the reading test. Although the income gap continues to narrow at the district level, the performance in 2006 and 2007 (3 percentage points) was unchanged.

High School Reading Gap

African American middle school students at the state level performed better than African American students in the Norfolk City Public School District on reading proficiency test in 2004 (−1) and 2005 (−2). The findings indicate that African American children at the state level scored 1 percentage point higher in narrowing the achievement gap than their district counterparts. However, this changed in 2005 and 2006 when African American students at the district level scored 2 and 3 percentage points higher respectively than their state peers in narrowing the reading gap. The internal district/internal state reading achievement gap has also narrowed between low-income and non-low-income students. In 2004, the low-income group performed 5 percentage points higher on the reading measures than their low-income state counterparts. In 2005, this group scored 8 percentage points above their state peers and 4 percentage points higher in 2007. This reflected a decline in narrowing the income gap between the district and state.

External Reading Gap: District Disadvantaged Versus State Advantaged

Elementary School Reading Gap

As indicated in Tables 7.1, 7.2, and 7.3, the Norfolk City Public School District's external gap for African American student was −16. This means that African American students in the district performed 16 percentage points below the state's advantaged group in 2004. However, these students closed the gap by 6 percentage points between 2004 and 2007. Between 2006 and 2007, the gap narrowed from −11 to −10, reflecting a 1-percentage-point decline in the gap. At the elementary level, the income gap between the district's disadvantaged students and the state's advantage students narrowed from −16 in 2004 to −11 in 2005 and 2006. It narrowed to −10 in 2007. Although a gap continues to exist in the income gap, it has narrowed over time.

Middle School Reading Gap

The reading achievement between the district's African American middle school students and state's advantaged students was –19 in 2004 and 2005; however, the gap increased in 2006 to –20 and decreased to –19 in 2007. These findings indicate that the gap between African American middle school students remained constant between 2004 and 2007. On the other hand, the income gap between low-income and non-low-income students increased from –17 percentage points in 2004 to –20 in 2007. This reflects an increase of 3 percentage increase; however, the gap between 2006 and 2007 remained the same (–20).

High School Reading Gap

The reading gap narrowed significantly between 2004 and 2007. In 2004, the group scored 12 percentage points below their advantaged counterparts in 2004. However, this increased by 3 percentage points (–15) in 2005, declined to –6 in 2006, and narrowed by 2 addition percentage points in 2007. Additionally, the low-income and non-low-income groups narrowed the reading gap from –9 percentage points in 2004 to –6 percentage points in 2007.

Mathematics Internal Gap

Elementary School Mathematics Gap

The mathematics achievement gap between African American and European American students in the district narrowed from –15 percentage points in 2004 to –11 in 2007. This reflects a decrease of 4 percentage points. It was also noted that the achievement gap between low-income and non-low-income elementary level students attending Norfolk City Public Schools increased by 2 percentage points between 2004 and 2007. In 2004, the gap was –15. This declined to –12 from 2005 to 2006 and declined to –11 in 2007. Overall the mathematics gap narrowed by 4 percentage points (See Tables 7.4, 7.5, and 7.6.)

Middle School Mathematics Gap

The mathematics achievement gap between African American and European American middle school students was –20 in 2004, –15 in 2005, –23 in 2006, and –23 in 2007. This reflected an increase of 3 percentage points between 2004 and 2007 in the mathematics proficiency gap. The income gap between low-income and non-low-income middle school students in the Norfolk City Public School District narrowed by 12 percentage points between 2004 and 2007. In 2004, the gap was –8 and –12 in 2005, and narrowed by 1 percentage from 2006 to 2007. High School The internal mathematics achievement gap between African American and European Ameri-

TABLE 7.4   Norfolk Elementary Mathematics Achievement Gaps 2004–2007

Elementary	2004	2005	2006	2007	2006–07 Change	Gap Closure Type
Internal District Gap						
African American/European American	–15	–12	–12	–11	1	1
Hispanic/European American	*	*	*	*	*	*
Low Income/Non-Low Income	–9	–8	–11	–11	1	1
Internal District vs. Internal state Gap						
African American/European American	2	3	3	2	–1	—
Hispanic/European American	*	*	*	*	*	*
Low Income/Non-Low Income	6	7	4	4	0	—
External Gap District Disadvantaged vs. State Disadvantaged						
African American/European American	–14	–11	–9	–10	–1	—
Hispanic/European American	*	*	*	*	*	*
Low Income/Non-Low Income	–11	–10	–10	–10	–1	—

Source: The Eli and Edythe Broad Foundation: Analysis of State Test Data (2008)
Notes:
   — indicates data not available
   * indicates calculation was not performed
   1 Both Advantaged and disadvantaged groups are increasing. The gap is closing
      because the disadvantaged group proficiencies are increasing at a faster rate than their
      disadvantaged counterparts.
   2 The gap is closing; however, proficiency for the advantaged group did not change or has
      declined.

can students was –14 in 2004, –18 in 2005, –13 in 2006 and –12 in 2007. This shows that the middle school mathematics gap narrowed by 2 percentage points between 2004 and 2007. Unfortunately, analysis of data indicated that the mathematics achievement gap between low-income and non-low-income students increased by 8 percentage points between 2004 and 2007. The mathematics gap was –2 in 2004, –6 in 2006 and –10 in 2007.

Internal District vs. Internal State Mathematics Gap

Elementary School Mathematics Gap

   As shown in Table 7.4, the internal district/internal state gap indicated that African American students in the school district of Norfolk, are doing

TABLE 7.5   Norfolk Middle School Mathematics Achievement Gaps 2004–2007

Middle	2004	2005	2006	2007	2006–07 Change	Gap Closure Type
Internal District Gap						
African American/European American	–20	–15	–23	–23	0	—
Hispanic/European American	*	*	*	*	*	*
Low Income/Non-Low Income	–8	–12	–21	–20	1	1
Internal District vs. Internal state Gap						
African American/European American	–2	4	2	0	–2	—
Hispanic/European American	*	*	*	*	*	*
Low Income/Non-Low Income	10	7	4	3	0	—
External Gap District Disadvantaged vs. State Disadvantaged						
African American/European American	–18	–16	–28	–29	–1	—
Hispanic/European American	*	*	*	*	*	*
Low Income/Non-Low Income	–15	–15	–28	–29	0	—

Source: The Eli and Edythe Broad Foundation: Analysis of State Test Data (2008)
Notes:
— indicates data not available
* indicates calculation was not performed
1 Both Advantaged and disadvantaged groups are increasing. The gap is closing
   because the disadvantaged group proficiencies are increasing at a faster rate than their
   disadvantaged counterparts.
2 The gap is closing; however, proficiency for the advantaged group did not change or has
   declined.

better than the state in narrowing the gap between their European American district counterparts and the state's African American students relative to European American students. In 2004, the gap was 2, suggesting that the district's African's American students are performing 2 percentage points above the state's African American students in narrowing the racial achievement gap. The district also did better than the state by 6 percentage points in 2005 and by 4 percentage points in 2006. However, by 2007, the district only outperformed the state by 2 percentage points. This represented a decrease (–2) in performance. A review of data indicated that low low-income income district elementary students narrowed the gap between their non-low-income peers at a faster rate than the state's low-income students. The mathematics gap was 6 percentage points in 2004, 8 in 2005, 5 in 2006, and 4 in 2007. The overall the gap narrowed by 2 percentage points during this time.

TABLE 7.6   Norfolk High School Reading Achievement Gaps 2004–2007

High	2004	2005	2006	2007	2006–07 Change	Gap Closure Type
Internal District Gap						
African American/European American	−14	−18	−13	−12	4	2
Hispanic/European American	*	*	*	*	*	*
Low Income/Non-Low Income	−2	*	−6	−10	−6	—
Internal District vs. Internal state Gap						
African American/European American	2	−3	0	−1	0	—
Hispanic/European American	*	*	*	*	*	*
Low Income/Non-Low Income	8	*	3	0	−7	—
External Gap District Disadvantaged vs. State Disadvantaged						
African American/European American	−13	−16	−14	−15	0	—
Hispanic/European American	*	*	*	*	*	*
Low Income/Non-Low Income	−7	*	−11	−14	−6	—

Source: The Eli and Edythe Broad Foundation: Analysis of State Test Data (2008)
Notes:
  — indicates data not available
  * indicates calculation was not performed
  1 Both Advantaged and disadvantaged groups are increasing. The gap is closing
    because the disadvantaged group proficiencies are increasing at a faster rate than their
    disadvantaged counterparts.
  2 The gap is closing; however, proficiency for the advantaged group did not change or has
    declined.

Middle School Mathematics Gap

Middle School African American students in the school district of Nor-folk, are doing better than the state in narrowing the gap between their European American district counterparts and the state's African American students relative to European American students. In 2004, the district and the state racial gaps were the same (0). In 2005 and 2006, the district outperformed the state by 2 percentage points. However, no difference was noted in mathematics proficiency between the two groups. The mathematics gap between the districts low-income students and non-low-income students indicates that middle school students outperformed the state in narrowing the gap. In 2004, the gap was 9, which suggested that the district's low-income middle school students performed 9 percentage points higher than their state counterparts in narrowing the mathematics gap. Findings also indicated that by 2007, the district low income students continued to outperform their state level counterparts in narrowing the income gap (−3).

High School Mathematics Gap

High School African American students in the school district of Norfolk, are narrowing the gap between their European American district counterparts and the state's African American students relative to European American students. In 2004, the gap was 2, suggesting that districts' African Americans outperformed those of the state in narrowing the high school mathematics gap between African American and European American students. The –3 indicates that the district performed 3 percentage points below the state in narrowing the gap. However, in 2006, the district and the state were the same (0) and that the state outperformed the district by 1 percent- age point in narrowing the gap in 2007. The district performed better in narrowing the mathematics income gap between low-income and non-low-income students. In 2004, the district outperformed the state by 8 percentage points, by 3 percentage points in 2005, and performed the same (0) as the state in 2007. This reflects a 3-percentage-point decline in narrowing the income gap between 2006 and 2007.

Mathematics External Gap: District Disadvantaged versus State Advantaged

Elementary School Mathematics Gap

The Norfolk City Public School District's external gap for elementary African American students in mathematics was –14. This means that African American students in the district performed 14 percentage points below the state's advantaged group in 2004. However, in 2005, the gap declined to –11 percentage points and –9 in 2006, and, increased to –10 in 2007. These findings indicate that the state outperformed the district in narrowing the achievement gap between Norfolk City Public Schools District's African American students and their European American peers. The district has closed this gap by 4 percentage points since 2004. At the elementary level, the income gap between the district's disadvantaged and the state's advantage students narrowed from –11 in 2004, to –10 from 2005–2007. Although data indicate that the state is performing better than the district in narrowing the income gap, the district gap did not increase.

Middle School Mathematics Gap

The mathematics achievement gap between the district's African American middle school students and state's advantaged students was –18 in 2004, –16 in 2005 , –28 in 2006, and –29 in 2007. These data indicate that the external middle school mathematics proficiency gap between African American middle school increased by 15 percentage points between 2004 and 2007. This significant gap increase suggests that African American district students are performing 29 percentage points below their state counterparts in narrowing the achievement gap. The state is outperforming the district in narrowing the mathematics achievement gap. Similar trends can be observed in the mathematics high school achievement gap. In 2004 2005, the income gap was −15; it increased to −28 in 2006 and increased 1 percentage point to −29 in 2007.

High School Mathematics Gap

The mathematics external gap was −13 in 2004, −16 in 2005, −14 in 2006, and − 15 in 2007. These trends reflect a 2-percentage-point increase in the mathematics proficiency gap between the district's African American students and the state's advantaged group. This gap increased by 1 percentage point between 2006 and 2007. As was the case at the middle school level, the external income gap increased from −7 in 2004 to −11 in 2006. The gap increased by 3 percentage points to −14 in 2007. These findings indicated that the state is outperforming the district in narrowing the income and racial achievement gaps in the Norfolk City Public School District.

CHAPTER 8

NARROWING ACHIEVEMENT GAPS

Successful Strategies from Norfolk Public Schools

Good schools, like good societies and good families, celebrate and cherish diversity.
—Deborah Meier, 1992

In a 2004 study funded by the North Central Regional Educational Laboratory, researchers examined a group of elementary schools that were narrowing the achievement gaps and compared them with a group of schools that were not narrowing the gaps. In this study, thirty-two schools were selected from six counties in the San Francisco Bay Area: Alameda, Contra Costa, Marin, San Francisco, San Mateo, and Santa Clara. Schools located in suburban, urban affluent and low socioeconomic areas were included in this study. Additionally, all racial and ethnic groups were included in the sample. The study focused on grades K–8. The findings indicated that the following factors were significant in narrowing the achievement gap: (a) *Professional Development.* Those who taught at the schools that narrowed the achievement gap were given more professional development in analyzing and interpreting data than their non-gap-narrowing counterparts; (b) *Encouragement from Leaders to use Inquiry.* Leaders in gap narrowing schools were more likely to encourage inquiry and analytical discussions about

Narrowing the Achievement Gap in a (Re)Segregated Urban School District, pages 127–137
Copyright © 2009 by Information Age Publishing

achievement gaps; (c) *Discussion of Data with Colleagues.* Individuals teaching in gap-narrowing schools were more likely to discuss the academic performance of African American and Latino students with their peers; (d) *Classroom Visitations.* Teachers in the gap-narrowing schools were more likely to visit the classrooms of their peers to observe instructional sequences; (e) *Teacher Collaboration.* Teachers from the gap-narrowing schools were more likely to request collaboration with their peers to share successful teaching strategies and to engage in reflective activities relevant to their instructional sequences (Legler, 2004). Specific recommendations emerging from data were: (a) Schools need to use frequent and reliable data. In other words, detailed information is needed so that teachers are able to participate in a continuous improvement process in charting student progress. This should not just take place once a year, but daily, weekly, and monthly. (b) Teachers need support to use data. That is, teachers need to be given opportunities to collaborate, reflect, discuss and to share instructional strategies. (c) Educators must understand that race matters. School districts should hire and promote minorities (Legler, 2004). Data indicated that schools narrowing the gaps have more minorities in leadership positions than their lagging-behind peer districts. Findings also indicated that teachers and administrators need to discuss race as an important factor in student performance and the reasons that achievement gaps exist (Legler, 2004). As Legler noted in his research findings:

> When we first disaggregated the data, people wanted to know, "Why we are disaggregating by race?" They said that we should be colorblind. But we replied we wanted to make sure that no pattern existed. It starts that way. You open up the level of conversations with small groups of teachers. If you share in a small group, experiences are shared. We purposefully made them mixed race. . . . We wanted to start small. We now have this group of teachers who have been empowered by these conversations, who now will speak up. They know that they have comrades who support them. It opens more doors. Conversations have become more honest. (Legler, 2004, p. 21)

The $1 million Broad Prize for Urban Education is awarded annually to urban school districts that have made the most progress in improving student performance by narrowing the achievement gaps across racial/ethnic groups and between high- and low-income students. The award is based on the factors listed below:

Meeting Federal No Child Left Behind Requirements

The No Child Left Behind Act (NCLB) requires schools to meet targets and goals in improving student performance. These targets must be achieved across all subgroups (race/ethnicity, income level, language, and disability). In 2004, 76 percent of the school in the district met Adequately Yearly Progress (AYP) as mandated by NCLB.

Consistent High Performance in Reading and Math while Reducing Achievement Gaps across Ethnic and Income Groups

When compared to other school districts in the state of Virginia with similar demographics, the district has been a consistent high performing system (2001–2004). As noted by the Broad prize methodology, Norfolk City Public School District outperformed comparable districts in the state in all six relevant areas: in reading and mathematics in elementary, middle and high schools. Analysis of data from the 2005 Broad Award indicated the following:

> The percentage of elementary students who reached proficiency in reading increased by 14 percentage points in the past four years, while middle school reading improved by 12 percentage points. The percentage of elementary students who reached proficiency in math increased by 14 percentage points in the past four years, while middle school math improved by 23 percentage points. Norfolk showed reductions in ethnic achievement gaps in the following categories: elementary reading for Hispanic students (11 percentage points) and middle school math for African American students (10 percentage points) when compared to their White counterparts. (Broad Foundation, 2008)

SUCCESSFUL PRACTICES AND PROGRAMS

The following practices were shown to be effective in the Norfolk Public Schools District in narrowing the achievement gap:

Curriculum Alignment and the Articulation of Academic Goals

The Standards of Learning for Virginia Public Schools establishes curriculum standard and assessments designed primarily to evaluate K–12 student academic achievement. Academic expectations are elaborated in the areas of English, mathematics, science, history, the fine arts, foreign language, health and physical education, driver education and technology. Specific objectives, instructional strategies, and technology-driven resources are provided for teachers.

Curriculum standards and assessments ground a rigorous accountability system. As the district noted:

> The district has assigned core-content teachers, department chairs, and grade-level leaders to help teachers fully align the curriculum. District instructional support specialists spend 70% of their time in classrooms helping teachers

implement the curriculum. District-wide quarterly assessments (and monthly assessments in some schools) are administered, and extensive walk-through observations are provided to struggling schools to ensure that the curriculum is being consistently implemented. (National Center for Educational Accountability, 2009, p. 2)

Staff Alignment and Capacity Building

The Norfolk City Public School District hires new principal primarily from with the district and has developed a Leadership Academy for new and existing principals. These administrators work with a local business consortium and the district in developing and enhancing leadership skills.

Norfolk increasingly relies on hiring principals from within the district's ranks. An academy coordinated with a local business consortium aims to develop and enhance leadership skills. The district also builds capacity by:

Recruiting minority teachers to reflect its student demographics. A citywide job fair allows the district to recruit and pre-screen hundreds of potential certified teacher applicants. An ethnic minority teacher network encourages discussion, provides role models, and offers tutorial input. The district has a formal three-tiered induction program designed to support teachers their first three years. The program is research-based and includes monthly activities for teachers, as well as a strong mentoring program (Broad Foundation, 2008, p. 3)

Centralized Instructional Programs and Practices

Instructional programs and practices are determined after careful review of data. Needs assessments are developed and the district then implements pilot programs to evaluate program effectiveness. Program effectiveness is linked directly to student achievement. The Norfolk City Public School District has centralized all academic programs and mandates the amount of time that must be devoted to the content areas. Even more crucial, the district is:

Focusing on the five dimensions of reading defined by the U.S. Department of Education, Norfolk has developed and implemented a web-based primary literacy program. The assessments allow the district to track the performance and reading deficiencies of every student in kindergarten and grades one and two. The district is planning to extend the program to grades three, four, and five, and eventually through high school. (http://www.broadprize.org/asset/2005_Norfolk.pdf)

Data-Driven Decision Making

The Norfolk City Public School District has implemented a three- tier Comprehensive Assessment' System (CAS) instrument designed to increase accountability across all levels, including the schools, central office departments, and the School Board. In utilizing the CAS, data are compared longitudinally over a five-year period. Tier I analyzes state and district level data, tier II examines school or department level data, and tier III details qualitative data elaborating the specific unit of analysis' accountability findings. The district also mandates quarterly benchmark assessments from K–12.

Additionally, approximately 90% of the district's schools issue monthly assessments. Teachers meet in teams to discuss the data and to plan instructional sequences. The district requires quarterly benchmark assessments in all grades. Ninety percent of Norfolk's schools have developed common assessments that teachers give monthly. Some schools are able to score their test sheets electronically on site so teachers and administrators can receive immediate feedback on student achievement.

Early Interventions and Adjustments

Those schools in the district not meeting the benchmark requirements are identified and given additional resources in the form support staff or increased funds to address deficits. These schools also receive assistance from outside teams who provide help in interpreting data and relevant instructional strategies. Additionally, a professional review board was established by the Norfolk City Public School District to work with teachers having problems meeting benchmarks or issues surrounding classroom management, organizational skills, and effective instructional strategies. The district also mandates in-school corrective programs for students not meeting specific benchmarks (http://www.broadprize.org/asset/2005_Norfolk.pdf).

Stable Leadership

In terms of system stability, the district contends that:

> Norfolk has had a continuity of leadership focused on a quality education for all children. John O. Simpson, who instituted the district's "All Means All" motto, served as superintendent from July 1998 until he retired in July 2004 when he handed the reins over to Denise K. Schnitzer, a 32-year veteran of the district. Schnitzer served as interim superintendent for one year. In July 2005, Stephen C. Jones was appointed Superintendent of Norfolk Public Schools. (http://www.broadprize.org/asset/2005_Norfolk.pdf)

Equity in Inputs and Outcomes

Educational equity is a concept that philosophically grounds educational practices and programs in American public schools. Unfortunately, not all actors in the education arena can agree on the definition of equity. Equity implies fairness in distributing services and resources according to individual differences and needs. This concept does not necessarily mean providing the identical services for each student. Inside and outside the classroom walls, it is obvious that providing the same services for all children can be deemed unfair. One must take individual needs into account because these needs may range from providing services and resources to the talented and gifted to the learning disabled, the physically challenged and others with individual needs. As is the case in the Norfolk district, schools must also show equal respect in providing services and resources to students. The allocation of funds, curricula, physical facilities, and integrated technology should not be provided to one group of students at the expense of another subgroup.

RECOMMENDATION FOR RESEGREGATED SCHOOL DISTRICTS

Educators must understand that excellence cannot flourish without fairness in the distribution and allocation of resources. Additionally, schools must maintain high standards, provide adequate governance. Furthermore, educators must show a positive relationship between costs and benefits, that is, efficiency should be a primary consideration. In becoming more efficient, schools should give more attention to inputs, throughputs and outputs. Accountability should be emphasized in terms of the final product: student achievement. Disadvantaged students are not limited to one race/ethnic group or geographical region. When we fail to provide a quality education for all children, the nation's economic stability becomes compromised and may result in higher crime rates and soaring health care costs. When equity and excellence are balanced, benefits are maximized for all children. It is obvious that when excellence and equity are in place in the schools, all members of society will benefit because the life chances for disadvantaged children will improve. In promoting and modeling equity, school leaders should consider the following:

High Expectations

All individuals working in school districts should be philosophically committed to the belief that all children can learn if they are given the appropriate opportunities and resources. Schools establish a school culture that models a belief in high expectations for all students across ethnic and socioeconomic boundaries. Expectations should be communicated to parents, students and all member of the school community. Students' work products should be displayed at the schools and incentives and recognition for academic achievement should be evident.

Shared Governance: Parental Involvement

In narrowing achievement gaps, school districts should develop strategies that will encourage parents of disadvantaged and advantaged students to participate in the schools decision-making process when appropriate. Schools must employ creative methods and strategies in increasing parental participation in schools. When parents feel that their input in curricula, after school and before school programs is valued, they are more likely to show more interest in the academic progress of their children. Local businesses, major corporations, local or even national celebrities can be used to attract parents and generate involvement. Schools must tap into strategies that are reflective of a changing landscape.

Hire Diverse Talented Teacher Leaders

School districts should hire teachers, principals, and other staff members who are knowledgeable about curricula, research, pedagogy, leadership, and can cross cultural boundaries in relating to students. The ability to see beyond skin color, race, ethnicity, and gender is essential for those committed to improving student achievement. High expectations are more than a concept; educators in the districts must model this daily. Additionally, districts should utilize talented tenured and non-tenured teachers in the primary grades and with special-needs students. In narrowing the achievement gap, talented teachers who are comfortable in diverse settings provide the key to success and they are needed more in the early grades to assist in preventing the gaps from growing.

Implement Rigorous Curricula and Goals

School districts should consider the global diversity within the classrooms. These diversities must be embraced when developing curricula and establishing goals and objectives. Diversity does not mean that one must compromise standards; however, it means that teachers should be able to connect students' background knowledge and learning styles to content. Higher order cognition and critical thinking skills should be a goal no matter the content area; therefore, it is important to understand students' experiences. This will better assist teachers in preparing for instruction by applying different curriculum delivery platforms. In providing instruction and selecting textbooks, district adoption committees should realize that all staff members must accept, internalize, and model the concept that equity and excellence are interrelated, that is, equity for disadvantaged students can only be achieved when excellence is achieved.

Utilize Data in Decision Making

Decisions relevant to improving the academic performance of students should use disaggregated student data to identify the need focus of instruction, to monitor progress, and to provide continuous feedback. It is also important to note that classroom teachers, district leaders, and policymakers should draw data from a variety of sources. These disaggregated data show student progress by student subgroups and should be utilized to analyze progress by gender, socioeconomic status, native language, ethnicity, and race. These data sources may include: state tests, norm-referenced tests, criterion reference tests, report cards, graduate rates, discipline reports, school safety reports, enrollment in advanced courses, etc. It is also essential that the data-driven accountability model provides frequent monitoring and feedback of students' progress. The data should guide instruction.

Implement Collaborative Professional Development Models

Professional development opportunities should be provided so that teachers, administrators, and other district level staff members will be able to meet and share experiences that directly relate to issues surrounding student achievement and narrowing achievement gaps Professional development opportunities should be provided so that teachers, administrators, and other district-level staff members will be able to meet and share experiences that directly relate to issues surrounding student achievement and narrowing achievement gaps. It is important to link professional development sequences to practice, research, and student learning. Teachers and teacher leaders should also be given opportunities to work collaboratively as they share and reflect upon their experiences with students. The ability to share success with colleagues and to engage in teacher classroom exchanges both add meaning to professional development. Professional development should also be used to assist teachers in better understanding a district's data- driven accountability process.

POLICY AGENDA RECOMMENDATIONS

Now that the Norfolk school district has resegregated, educators must move beyond considering desegregation as a viable variable in narrowing the achievement gap. Districts must take a page out of Norfolk's book and focus more on variables and characteristics that affect the achievement gaps in their schools. More rigorous accountability systems are needed not just for teachers, but for every individual residing in the district. We must all play a role in narrowing the achievement gaps between and among subgroups. The United States Supreme Court has spoken and, given the changing demographics, desegregated schools may become dinosaurs. It is time to look beyond resegregation and focus on improving the life chances of students who attend these segregated institutions. We as a nation can do better and should do better in educating our children. In order to expand educational opportunities and to narrow the achievement gaps among diverse groups, the following policy recommendations are proposed:

NATIONAL POLICY AGENDA

Since there is no longer a commitment from the federal court to integrate the nation's public schools, education reformers policymakers at all governmental levels, and advocacy groups must assume key roles in decision making and policy development relevant to governing resegregated schools. This should be reflected in monitoring education reform policies coming from the members of Congress and the United States Department of Education. It is also important to remember that the lack of activism that characterized the federal government's involvement in desegregation initiatives in the 1980s has followed us into the twenty-first century.

Given the fact that we must educate and challenge all students, researchers and policy makers must continue to identify those variables that are most significant in improving academic performance and narrowing achievement gaps. In addressing the above, national agenda should focus on school finance equity and school district governance and should require all policy proposals to view education as a civil right. The United States Department of Education should view the academic achievement of African American males as a national crisis and require more extensive accountability measures specifically focused on this problem. Perhaps the model in place in the Virginia Beach City Schools aimed at narrowing the achievement gap between African American males and non-African American males should be examined more carefully and, where appropriate, applied to other school districts.

STATE POLICY AGENDA

Although the United States Supreme Court has ruled that race can no longer be utilized as a factor in assigning students to public schools, school leaders should use technology to create virtually desegregated schools. As educators, we can integrate resegregated classrooms and schools creatively and virtually. State education agencies should form collaborative structures with colleges and universities, funding agencies, and corporate entities to assist in developing teaching and learning environments that are technology centered.

In narrowing the achievement gap, governors, legislators, and state agencies should ensure that adequate resources are provided to these learning centers and that rigorous accountability is shared among school leaders, teachers, students, the community, and the family. Appropriate resources and services should be provided to all students based upon their needs. Those schools located in urban and rural areas should be funded at higher levels than many of their more affluent suburban counterparts. Urban and rural centers are more likely to have more special-need students; therefore, fiscal equity becomes a crucial policy issue. The states' formulas for funding local districts should not impose unfair burdens on selected disadvantaged student groups. Federal and state funding sources that are designed to provide enrichment opportunities for students should be examined as possible avenues to additional resources.

State departments of education should require local school districts to develop and implement plans designed specifically to narrow the achievement gaps between African American males and all other subgroups.

LOCAL/URBAN POLICY AGENDA

Local boards of education should require school districts to examine alternative governance models with technology at the center. Science and technology competencies must be viewed as essential to providing a quality education for all students. Disadvantaged students must be challenged in mathematics and the sciences. High expectations for all students must be carefully balanced and modeled by teachers and those in leadership positions. School districts should consider this a primary factor in granting tenure to teachers.

Colleges and universities should develop teacher preparation programs that emphasize a culturally responsive curriculum that requires students to participate in a two-year teaching internship in the public schools. Additionally, these institutions should redesign curricula to reflect the needs of a culturally and structurally diverse society.

The higher-education professors should be required to hold selected classes in public school districts and to work more closely with districts and local community agencies in developing and conducting professional development activities. Professional development should also include sessions on instructional strategies aimed at reducing the achievement gap between African American males and other subgroups.

REFERENCES

Access Quality Education: Connecticut Litigation (2009). Retrieved March 1, 2009 from http://www.schoolfunding.info/states/ct/lit_ct.php3.

Anderson, L. (1966). *The effect of desegregation on the achievement and personality patterns of negro children.* Unpublished Doctoral Dissertation. George Peabody College for Teachers. University Microfilms, 66-11237. 27, 1529A.

Annual Report on the Condition and Needs of Public Schools in Virginia, (November 26, 2003). Richmond Virginia: Virginia Board of Education.

Aptheker, H. (1969). *The history of the negro people in the United States.* New York: International.

Armor, D. (1972) School and family effects on black and white achievement: A re-examination of USOE data. In F. Mosteller (Ed.), *On equality of educational opportunity* (pp. 167–229). New York: Random House.

Armor, D. (1981), White flight and the future of school desegregation. In W. G. Stephan & J. R. Feagan (Eds.). *School desegregation: Past, present and future.* New York: Plenum.

Bailey, K. (2008). *Closing the achievement gap for African American males.* Norfolk City Public Schools, VA: Department of Testing and Statistics.

Baker, J. (1962). Integration in Virginia schools. *Virginia Journal of Education, 56*, 18.

Bailey, K. (2008) *Closing the achievement gap for African American males. Norfolk City Public Schools.* Norfolk, VA: Department of Testing and Statistics.

Balfanz, R., & Legters, N. (2004). *Locating the dropout crisis.* Baltimore, MD: Johns Hopkins University, Center for Social Organization of Schools.

Bardolph, R. (Ed.) (1970). *The civil rights record: Black America and the law.* New York: Thomas Crowell.

Barnes, C. A. (1983). *Journey from Jim Crow.* New York: Columbia University Press.

Barth, A. (1974). *Prophets of honor: Great dissents and great dissenters in the supreme court.* New York: Knopf.

Narrowing the Achievement Gap in a (Re)Segregated Urban School District, pages 139–148
Copyright © 2009 by Information Age Publishing

Beating the Odds VIII: (2008). An analysis of student performance and achievement gaps on state assessments. Results from the 2006–2007 School Year. Retrieved March 1, 2009 from: http://www.cgcs.org/publications/achievement.aspx

Bliss, J. (1991). *Rethinking effective schools research and practice.* Englewood Cliffs, NJ: Prentice Hall.

Board of Education of Oklahoma City v. Dowell, (1990). 498 U.S. 237 (1991)

Boehner, J. (August 28, 2001). *News from the committee.* Retrieved March 12, 2009 from Washington, D.C. U.S. Department of Education.

Brewer v. School Board of City of Norfolk Virginia E (1970). 456 F.2d 943.

Bridge, R. G., Judd, C. M., & Mock, P. R. (1979). *The determinants of educational outcomes: The impact of families, peers, teachers, and schools.* Cambridge, MA: Harper and Row.

Britzman, D. P. (1998). Cultural myths in the making of a teacher: Biography and social structure in teacher education. *Harvard Educational Review, 56*(4), 442–455.

Broad Award. (2005). Retrieved June 30, 2009 from http://www.broadmedical. org/funding/funded_grants/2005.html. Los Angeles, CA, The Eli and Edyth Broad Foundation.

Broad Foundation. (2008). Retrieved June 30, 2009 from http://www.broadfoundation.org Los Angeles, CA, The Eli and Edyth Broad Foundation.

Bronte, C. (2003). *Jayne Eyre.* New York: Penguin Classics.

Brown, v. Topeka, Kansas Board of Education, (1954) 347 U.S. 483, 74 S. Ct. 686, 98 L. Ed. 873, 3ay 17, 1954.

Brown II v. Topeka, Kansas Board of Education, (1955) 349 U.S. 294, 75 S. Ct. 753, 99 L. Ed.(1955) .

Burger, M. (April, 1983). Neighborhood Schools. *Urban Education,* 7–28.

Burton, N., & Jones L. V. (1982) Recent trends in achievement levels of black and white youths. *Educational Researcher, 11*(4), 10–14, 17.

Campbell, E. (1960). *When a city closes its schools.* Chapel Hill: University of North Carolina Press.

Carey, K. (2004). *The funding gap 2004: Many states still shortchange low-income and minority students.* Washington, DC: The Education Trust.

Carr, L. and Zeigler, D. (October, 1990) White flight and white return in Norfolk: A test of predictions. *Sociology of Education, 63,* 272–282.

Census Tracts (1980) Norfolk–Virginia Beach–Portsmouth, Virginia. Census of Population and Housing. Washington D.C.: United States Department of Commerce, Bureau of Census.

Cohen, D. (November, 1967) School desegregation and white achievement. In *Papers prepared for the National Conference on Equal Educational Opportunities in American Cities* (pp. 279–304), Washington D.C.: U.S. Commission on Civil Rights.

Cohen, D., Pettigrew, T., & Riley, R. (1972), Race and the outcomes of schooling. In F. Mosteller & D. Moynihan (Eds.), *On equality of educational opportunity* (pp. 343–368). New York: Random House.

Cohen, D., Gintis, H., Heyns, N., & Michelson, S. (1972). *Inequality: A reassessment of the first effect of family and schooling in America.* New York: Basic Books.

Coleman, J. (1966). *Equality of educational opportunity.* Washington, D.C.: U.S. Department of Health, Education and Welfare, Office of Education.

Chubb, J., & Hanushek, E. (1990). Reforming education reform. In H. J. Aaron & R. D. Reischauer (Eds.), *Setting National Priorities: Budget choices for the next century* (pp. 213–247). Washington, D.C.: The Brookings Institute.

Civil Rights Monitor. (1986). Vol 1 #4 p. 1. Retrieved February 15, 2009 from http://www.civilrights.org/publications/monitor/march1986/art6p1.htm

Collins, M. (February, 2006) *For teachers and leaders.* Retrieved June 30, 2009 from http://www.motivateus.com/teach58.htm.

Comer, J. (June 26, 2001). *Closing the achievement gap.* african.com WebSite. Koret Communications Limited. Microsoft Corporation.

Clotfelter, C. T. (2004). *After Brown: The rise and retreat of school desegregation.* Princeton, NJ: Princeton University Press.

Coleman, J. (1966). *Equality of educational opportunity.* Washington, D.C.: U.S. Department of Health, Education and Welfare, Office of Education.

Council of Great City Schools. (2008). *Beating the odds: City by city profiles.* Washington, D.C. Council of Great City Schools.

Covert, J. (1890). *The race problem.* Retrieved March 1, 2009, from http://www.maquah.net/Historical/Mohonk.html. Washington, D.C. Government Printing Office. pp. 31–32.

Crain, R. (1971). School integration and academic achievement of negroes. *Sociology of Education, 44*(1), 1–26.

Cubberly, E. (1947). *Public education in the United States.* Cambridge, Massachusetts: Mifflin Company.

Cummings v. Board of Education of Richmond County, 175 U.S. 528 (1899).

Davis, A. (1939). The socialization of the American Negro child and adolescent. *Journal of Negro Education, 8,* 264–274.

Davis, A. (1948). *Social-class influences upon learning.* Cambridge, MA: Harvard University Press.

Davis, A. (1951). How does cultural bias in intelligence tests arise? In K. Eells, A. Davis, R. Havighurst, V. Herrick, & R. Tyler, (Eds.). *Intelligence and cultural differences* (pp. 45–62). Chicago: University of Chicago Press.

Davis, A., & Eells, K. (1953). *Davis–Eells test of general intelligence.* Chicago: The University of Chicago Press.

Davis, J. (1973). *Busing in southern schools: An evaluation of the effects of the emergency assistance program and of desegregation.* Chicago: National Opinion Research Center.

Deemer, S. A. (2004). Classroom goal orientation in high school classrooms: Revealing links between teacher beliefs and classroom environment. *Educational Research, 46*(1), 73–90.

Doyle, M. (Winter 2005). From desegregation to resegregation: Public schools in Norfolk, Virginia 1954–2002. *The Journal of African American History, 90*(1/2), 64–83.

Education Association of Norfolk May 18, 1983. Desegregation Notes: Norfolk, Virginia. Education Association of Norfolk. 5/18/83.

Eli and Edythe Broad Foundation: The 2008 Broad Prize for Urban Education. Retrieved March 1, 2009 from http://www.broadprize.org/asset/1214-summarydataandanalysisprocedures.pdf

Ely, J. (May 1976). *The crisis of conservative Virginia.* Knoxville, Tennessee: The University of Tennessee Press.

Epstein, L., & Walker, T. G. (1995). The role of the supreme court in American society: Playing the reconstruction game. In L. Epstein (Ed.). *Contemplating courts.* Washington, DC: Congressional Quarterly Press.

Evans, R. (April 2004). *Reframing the achievement Gap.* Phi Delta Kappan. Retrieved March 2, 2009 from http://findarticles.com/p/articles/mi_6952/is_8_86/ai_n28266608

Fahim, M. (2005). *Additional revenue sources are hard to find as US cities face increased responsibilities.* Retrieved February 1, 2009 from http://www.citymayors.com/finance/finance_uscities_2.html

Ferguson, H., & Plaut, R. (April, 1954). Talent to develop or to lose. *Education Record.* 138.

Forgione, P. (1998). *Achievement in the United States: Progress since A Nation at Risk?* Center For Education Reform and Empower America: Washington, D.C.: U.S. Commissioner of Education Statistics, National Center for Education Statistics, Office of Educational Research and Improvement. United States Department of Education.

Fortenberry, J. (1959). The achievement of negro public in mixed and non-mixed schools. Doctoral dissertation, University of Oklahoma. Unpublished Dissertation. Norman: The University of Oklahoma.

Frary, R., & Goolsby, T. (1970). Achievement of integrated and segregated negro and white first graders in a southern city. *Integrated Education, 8,* 34–41.

Freeman v. Pitts (89-1290), 498 U.S. 1081 (1992).

Gaines ex rel Missouri v. Canada. (1938). 305 U.S. 337.

Gerald, H., & Miller, N. (1975). *School desegregation.* New York: Plenum Press.

Green v. County School Board of New Kent County, 391 U.S. 430, 88 S. Ct. 1689, 20 L Ed. 2d 716 (1968).

Greene, J. P., & Winters, M. (2005). *Leaving boys behind: Public high school graduation rates.* New York: Manhattan Institute for Policy Research.

Guthrie, J. (1970). A survey of school effectiveness studies. In *Do teachers make a difference?* Washington D.C.: U.S. Department of Health, Education, and Welfare.

Haskins, R., & Rouse, C. (2005). *Closing achievement gaps. Policy briefs.* Retrieved January 12, 2009 from http://www.futureofchildren.org/usr_doc/Policy_Brief__SPRING_2005pdf.pdf

Haycock, K. (2001). Helping all students advance. *Educational Leadership, 62*(3), 70–73.

Hayes, E. (1981). *Busing and desegregation.* Springfield, Illinois: Charles C. Thomas.

Hedges, L. V., Laine, R. D., & Greenwald, R. (1994). Does money matter? A meta analysis of studies of the effects of differential school inputs on student outcomes. *Educational Researcher 23*(3), 5–14.

Hedges, L., & Nowell, A. (April, 1999). Changes in the black–white achievement gap test scores. *Sociology of Education, 72*(2) 111–135.

Hershman, J. Jr. (1998). Massive resistance meets its match: The emergence of a pro-public majority. In D. Lassiter & A. Lewis (Eds.), *The moderate's dilemma: Massive resistance to school desegregation in Virginia* (pp. 114–115). Charlottesville: University Press of Virginia.

Heubert, J. (1999). *Law and school reform.* Connecticut: Yale University Press.

Holzman, M. (2004). *Public education and black male students: A state report card.* The Schott Educational Inequity Index, Cambridge, MA. The Foundation for Public Education.

Jencks, C., & Brown, M. (1975). *The effects of desegregation on student achievement: Some new evidence from Equality of Opportunity of Education Survey.* Center for Education Policy Research. Cambridge, MA: Harvard Graduate School of Education.

Jencks, C., Smith, M., Acland, H., Bane, M. J., Cohen, D., Gintis, H., Heynes, B., & Michelson, S. (1972). *Inequality: A reassessment of the effect of family and schooling in America.* New York: Harper and Row.

Jewell-Jackson, D. (1996). *Ending mandatory busing for desegregation in Norfolk, Virginia: A case study explaining the decision making process in a formerly de jure southern school district.* (Ph.D. diss., Harvard Graduate School of Education, 1995). In addition, see, Susan E. Eaton and Christina Meldrum, "Broken Promises: Resegregation in Norfolk, Virginia," in Dismantling Desegregation, ed. Gary Orfield and Susan Eaton New York: The New Press.

Klein, Z., & Eshel, Y. (1977). Towards a psychosocial definition of school integration, *Megamot, 23,* 17–40.

Kousser, J., & McPherson, J. (1982). *Region, race, and reconstruction: Essays in honor of C. Vann Woodward,* New York: Oxford University Press.

Kozol, J. (1996). *Amazing grace: Lives of children and the conscience of a nation.* New York: Harper Perennial.

Krol, R. (1979). *A meta analysis of comparative research on the effects of desegregation on academic achievement.* Doctoral Dissertation at Michigan University. Kalamazoo, Michigan.

Laurent, J. (1969). *Effects of race and racial balance of schools on academic achievement performance.* Unpublished Doctoral Dissertation. University of Oregon, Eugene Oregon.

Lee, V., & Burkam, D. (2002). *Inequality at the starting gate: Social background differences in achievement as children begin school.* Washington, D.C.: Economic Policy Institute.

Leflar R., & Davis W. (1954). Segregation in the public schools. *Harvard Law Review, 377,* 430–435.

Legler, R. (2004). *Perspectives on the achievement gap: Fostering the academic success of minority and low income students.* Naperville, IL. Learning Point Associates.

Lemke, E. (1979). The effects of busing on the achievement of white and black students. *Educational Studies, 9,* 409–415.

Lesser, G. (1964). *Some effects of segregation and desegregation in the schools.* Washington, D.C. ERIC Document. ED002316.

Levy, L., & Phillips, H. (1951). The Roberts case: Source of the separate but equal doctrine. *American Historical Review, 56,* 510–518.

Logan, J. (April 26, 2004). *Resegregation in American public schools? Not in the 1990s.* Lewis Mumford Center For Comparative Urban Regional Research: University at Albany.

Love, A., & Kruger, A. C. (2005). Teacher beliefs and student achievement in Urban schools serving African American students. *Journal of Educational Research, 99*(2), 87–98.

MacKenzie J. (1984). quoted in *Riddick v. School Board of the City of Norfolk,* 627 F. Supp, 814, 819 (U.S. Dist. 1984). See also Eaton, "Broken Promises," 117.

Mahard, R., & Crain, R. (1978). Desegregation and black achievement: A review of research. *Law and Contemporary Problems, 42,* 7–56.

Matzen, S. (1965). *The relationship between racial composition and scholastic achievement in elementary schools.* Palo Alto, CA: Unpublished Doctoral Dissertation, Stanford University.

Mayer, R. (1973). *The impact of school desegregation in a southern city.* Lanham, MD: Lexington Books.

McAndrews, L. (1998). The politics of principle: Richard Nixon and school desegregation. *The Journal of Negro History, 83*(3), 187–200.

McGuire, C. K. (1990). Business involvement in the 1990s. In D. Mitchell & M. Goertz (Eds.), *Education politics for the new century* (pp. 107–118). Philadelphia: The Falmer Press.

McGuire, C. K. (2008). Meeting the challenges of urban communities. In C. K. McGuire & V. W. Ikpa (Eds.), *Policy leadership and student achievement: Implications for urban communities* (pp. 3–16). Charoltte, NC: Information Age.

McLaurin v. Oklahoma State Regents for Higher Education. (1950). 70 S.Ct. 851, 339 U.S. 637, 94 L.Ed. 1149

McPartland, J. (1968). *The segregated student in desegregated schools: Sources of influence on negro school students.* Baltimore, MD: The Johns Hopkins University Press.

Meier, D. (1992). *New York educational leadership and accountability.* Retrieved July 1, 2009 from http://donnacooke.com/deborah_meier.htm.

Milliken v. Bradley, (1974) 418 U.S. 717.

Muse, B. (1961). *Virginia's massive resistance.* Bloomington: University of Indiana Press.

Narot, R. (1973) *Teacher prejudice and teacher behavior in desegregated schools: An evaluation of the effects of emergency school assistance programs and desegregation.* Chicago: Chicago National Research Center.

National Assessment of Educational Progress. (2000). *The nation's report card.* Washington, D.C.: United States Department of Education.

National Assessment of Educational Progress. (2007). *The nation's report card.* Washington, D.C.: United States Department of Education.

National Center for Education Statistics. (2006). *The NCES common core of data (CCD). Public elementary/secondary school universe survey.* U.S. Department of Education, 1993–94, 2000–01 and 2003–04.

National Center for Education Statistics. (2007). *NAEP, Summary data tables, National. The nation's report card.* Retrieved March 1, 2008 from http://nces.ed.gov. Washington, DC: United States Department of Education.

National Center for Education Statistics. (2008). *NAEP, Summary data tables.* Washington, D.C. : United States Department of Education.

National Center for Educational Accountability. (2009). Retrieved March 2, 2009 from: http://www.just4kids.org/en/

National League of Cities 19th Annual Survey. (2003). Washington, DC.: National League of Cities.

Neild, R. C., & Balfanz, R. (2001). *An extreme degree of difficulty: The educational demographics of the ninth grade in Philadelphia.* Baltimore MD: Johns Hopkins University Center for Social Organization of Schools.

No Child Left Behind. (2002). PUBLIC LAW 107–110—JAN. 8, 2002 115 STAT. 1425. Washington D.C.: United States Department of Education.

Norfolk Census Tracts. (1980). Norfolk–Virginia Beach–Portsmouth, Virginia. Census of Population and Housing. Washington D.C.: United States Department of Commerce, Bureau of Census.

Norfolk Census Tracts. (2000). Norfolk–Virginia Beach–Portsmouth, Virginia. Census of Population and Housing. Washington D.C.: United States Department of Commerce, Bureau of Census.

Norfolk City Schools Special Report on Enrollment. (October 1, 1968). Norfolk Public Schools, Office of the Chief Operating Officer, File Cabinet for Busing, Transportation Folder.

Norfolk Public Schools. (2008). *Service matters.* Retrieved June 30, 2009 from http://www.schoolmatters.com/schools.aspx/q/page=dp/did=4096.

Norfolk Public School District: Division Report: Executive Summary. (2006). Norfolk Public Schools Division Report 2004–2005. Norfolk, Virginia Norfolk City Schools. pp. 1–75.

Obama, B. (March 11, 2009). *Transcript: Obama speaks to the United States hispanic chamber of commerce.* Retrieved March 15, 2009 from http://voices.washingtonpost.com/x-equals-why/2009/03/obama_on_math_education.html?hpid=sec-education

Odden, A., Goetz, M., & Picus, L. (2007, March 14). *Paying for school finance adequacy with the national average per pupil expenditures.* Seattle: University of Washington, Working Paper 2.

Ogbu, J. (1998). Voluntary and involuntary minorities: A cultural-ecological theory of school performance with some implications for education. *Anthropology and Education Quarterly, 29,* 155–188.

Orfield, G. (2009) *The civil rights project: School resegregation and civil rights challenges for the Obama administration: A new report from the civil rights project at UCLA.* Retrieved June 30, 2009 from http://www.civilrightsproject.ucla.edu/news/pressreleases/pressrelease20090114-report.pdf.

Orfield, G., Bachmeier, D., James, D., & Eitle, T. (1997). Deeping segregating in American public schools: A special report from the Harvard project on school desegregation. *Equity & Excellence in Education, 30*(2), 5–24.

Orfield, G., & Eaton, S. (1996). *Dismanteling desegregation: The quiet reversal of Brown v. Board of Education.* New York: The New Press.

Orfield, G., & Lee, C. (August, 2007). *Historic reversals, accelerating resegregation, and the need for new integration strategies. A report of the civil rights project.* Paper presented at UCLA.

Orfield, G., & Lee, C. (2005). *Why segregation matters: Poverty and educational inequality.* Cambridge, MA: The Civil Rights Project at Harvard University.

O'Riley R. (1970). *Racial and social isolation in the schools.* New York: Praeger.

Pagano, M. (2003). *Cities fiscal challenges continue to worsen in 2003.* Washington, DC: Research Briefs, National League of Cities.

Parents Involved in Community Schools v. Seattle School District. 05-908 and 05-915, 2007.

Pettigrew, T., & Pajonas, P. (1964). *Social psychological considerations of racially balanced schools.* Unpublished working paper prepared for the New York State Commissioner of Education. New York: New York Commisioner of Education.

Peabody, G. (2002). *The Tennessee historical society.* Retrieved June 30, 2009 from http://tennesseeencyclopedia.net/imagegallery.php?EntryID=G012.

Phillips, L., & Bianchi, W. (January, 1975). Desegregation, reading, achievement and problem behavior in two elementary schools, *Urban Education, 9*(4), 325–339.

Planty, M., & Devoe, J. (2005). *An examination of the conditions of school facilities attended by 10th-grade students in 2002* (NCES 2006-302). Washington, DC: U.S. Government Printing Office.

Plessy v. Ferguson (1896). 163 U.S. 537.

Pride, R., & Woodard, D. (1985). *The burden of busing.* Knoxville: University of Tennessee Press.

Purl, M. (1969). *The effect of integration on the achievement of elementary pupils: A progress report.* Unpublished manuscript, Riverside, CA: Riverside Unified School District.

Purl, M., & Dawson, J. (1971). *The achievement of pupils in desegregated schools.* Riverside CA: Riverside Unified School District.

Raffel, J. (1998). *A historial dictionary of school segregation and desegregation: The American experience.* Westport, CT: Greenwood Press.

Rankin, S. (1972). *Shaker Heights school board study. (February, 1972). An interim evaluation of the Shaker Heights school plan.* Shaker Heights, OH: Shaker Heights School District.

Rawls, J. (1999). *Justice as fairness.* Cambridge, MA: Harvard University.

Riddick v. School Board of the City of Norfolk, (1984a). 627 F. Supp, 814, 816 (U.S. Dist. 1984).

Riddick. v. School Board of the City of Norfolk, (1986b). 784 F. 2d 521, 527 (4th Cir. 1986).

Rist, R. (1970) Student social class and teacher expectations: The self fulfilling prophecy in ghetto education. *Harvard Educational Review, 35*, 389–400.

Roberts v. City of Boston. (1849). 59 Mass. 198, 5 Cush. 198.

Rooney, P., et al. (2006). *The condition of education 2006* (NCES 2006-071). Washington, DC: U.S. Government Printing Office.

Rossell, C., & Hawley, W. (1983). *The consequences of school desegregation.* Philadelphia: Temple University Press.

Rotunda, R. (1993). *Modern constitutional law: Cases and notes.* St. Paul, MN: West Publishing.

Samuels, I. (1958). *Desegregated education and differences in academic achievement.* Unpublished Doctoral Dissertation, Bloomington: University of Indiana.

Schellenberg, J., & Halteman, J. (1976). Busing and academic achievement: A two year follow-up. *Urban Education, 10*(4), 357–365.

References ▪ **147**

Schultz, S. K. (1973). *The culture factory: Boston public schools, 1789–1860.* New York: Oxford University Press.

Smith, T. P. (1849, October 5). Vindication. *The Liberator, 19,* 160.

Sipuel v. Board of Regents of the University of Oklahoma (1948) 332 U.S. 631 (1948)

Shaw, M. (1973). Changes in sociometric choices following forced integration of an elementary school. *Journal of Social Issues, 29*(4) 143–157.

St. John, N., & Lewis, R. (1971). The influence of school racial context on academic achievement. *Social Problems, 19,* 68–78.

St. John, N. (1975). *School desegregation outcome for children.* New York: Wiley.

Swann v. Charlotte-Mecklenburg Board of Education (1971), 402 U.S. 1, 91 S. Ct. 1267, 28 L. Ed. 2d 554 (1971).

Swann, C., & Dyuduk, Y. (2006). *Task force on poverty, work, and opportunity open to new approaches to old problem.* Retrieved June 30, 2009 from http://usmayors.org/ usmayornewspaper/documents/04_10_06/poverty.asp.

Sweatt v. Painter 339 U.S. 629, (1950.)

The Condition of Education. (2000). *Findings from the condition of education 2000.* Washington, D.C.: National Center for Education Statistics on the Rise Retrieved January 2, 2006 from: http://nces.ed.gov/programs.

The Condition of Education. (2008). *Findings from the condition of education 2008: Enrollment, student diversity.* Washington, D.C: National Center for Education Statistics on the Rise. Retrieved March 2, 2009 from http://nces.ed.gov/programs/coe/.

The Nation's Report Card. (2007). Retrieved June 30, 2009 from: http://nationsreportcard.gov/. NAEP, Washington, D.C.

Teel, J. E., Jackson, E., & Mayo, C. (1967). Family experiences in Operation Exodus. In U.S. Commission on Civil Rights, Hearings Held in Boston, Massachusetts. Washington, D.C. Government Printing office, Department of Health education and Welfare.

U.S. Census Bureau. (2004). U.S. interim projections by age, sex, race, and Hispanic origin. Retrieved March 1, 2009 from http://www.census.gov/ipc/www/usinterimproj

U.S. Conference of Mayors Status Report on Hunger and Homeless Survey. (2007). Retrieved June 30, 2009 from: http://usmayors.org/HHSurvey2007/hhsurvey07.pdf. Washington, D.C.: United States Conference of Mayors.

United States Commission on Civil Rights. (1977). *Reviewing a decade of school desegregation. 1966–1977. Survey of School Superintendents.* Washington D.C.: United States Department of education.

U.S. Department of Education, National Center for Education Statistics. (2005). *The nation's report card: Reading 2005* (NCES 2006-451). Washington, DC: U.S. Government Printing Office.

U.S. Department of Education, Office of Vocational and Adult Education. (2002). *Adult Education and Family Literacy Act Report to Congress on State Performance.* Washington, D.C.: U. S. Department of Education, Office of Vocational and Adult and Vocational Education.

Virginia Beach City Public Schools. (November, 2008). *Improving the Academic Performance of African American Males: A Progress Report.* Retrieved March 1, 2008 from: http://www.vbschools.com/school_data/AcademicPerf1108.pdf

Weinberg, M. (1968). *Desegregation research: An appraisal.* Bloomington, IN: Phi Delta Commission.

Weinberg, M. (1971). *Desegregation research: An appraisal, special edition.* Bloomington, IN: Phi Delta Commission.

Weinberg, M. (1977). *A chance to learn.* Boston: Cambridge University Press.

Weinberg, M. (1983). *The search for quality integrated education.* Westport, CT: Greenwood Press.

Weiss, S. (March, 2003). *The progress of education, Reform 2003: Closing the achievement gap.* New York: Education Commission of the States. Vol 4, No. 1.

Wexler, S. (1993). *The civil rights movement.* New York: Facts on File.

Wise, A., & Gendler, T. (1989). Rich schools, poor schools. *The College Board Review, 151,* 12–37.

Wilson, A. (1967). *Educational consequences of segregation in a California community. Racial isolation in the Public Schools.* Vol. 11. Washington, D.C.: Government Printing Office, Department of Health education and Welfare.

Winkler, D. (1975). Educational Achievement and School Peer Group Composition. *The Journal of Human Resources, 10*(2), 189–204. Madison: University of Wisconsin Press. Retrieved February 22, 2009 from http://www.jstor.org/stable/144826.

Wirt, J., Rooney, P., Choy, S., Provasnik, S., Sen, A., & Tobin, R. (2004). *The condition of education 2004* (NCES 2004-077). Washington, DC: U.S. Government Printing Office.

Woodward, C. (1966). *The strange career of Jim Crow.* London: Oxford University Press.

Woodson, C. (1919). *The education of the negro to 1861: The education of the negro: A history of the education of the colored people of the United States from the beginning of slavery to the Civil War.* Reprint, New York: Arno Press, 1968.

Wrightstone, J., McClelland, S., & Forlano, G. (1966). *Evaluation of the community zoning program.* New York: Bureau of Educational Research.

Zirkel, P., & Moses, E. G. (1971). Self concept and Ethnic group membership among public school students. *American Educational Research Journal, 8*(2), 253–265.

Variables	Beta	T	Significance of T
Percentage African American students	−.22916	−1.464	.1445
Percentage with advanced degrees	−.01041	−.086	.9314
Substitute expenditures	−.10450	−1.093	.2757
Age of school building	−.13800	−2.040	.0426
Library books	.05648	.695	.4879
Average teacher salary	−.33555	−2.829	.0051
Instructional expenditures	−.06029	.678	.4928
School income	−.20118	2.187	.0298
Percentage African American teachers	.16991	1.532	.1269
Student–Teacher ratio	−.01539	−.124	.9013
Average class size	.02628	.230	.8392
(Constant)		2.307	.0202

Narrowing the Achievement Gap in a (Re)Segregated Urban School District, pages 149–170
Copyright © 2009 by Information Age Publishing
149

APPENDIX B:
Selected Multiple Regression Statistics
School Characteristics
All Female Students

Variables	Beta	T	Significance of T
Percentage African American students	−.16527	−1.128	.2608
Substitute expenditures	.07503	.739	.4606
Percentage with advanced degrees	−.08356	−.750	.4545
Age of school building	−.02040	−.283	.7776
School income	−.25002	2.768	.0062
Instructional expenditures	.17990	1.8959	.0645
Percentage African American teachers	−.10356	−.992	.3222
Average class size	−.02811	−.234	.8151
Average teacher salary	−.22144	−2.086	.0383
Library books	.28178	2.289	.0232
Student–Teacher ratio	.04010	.309	.7573
(Constant)		1.563	.1196

APPENDIX C:
Selected Multiple Regression Statistics
School Characteristics
All Students

Variables	Beta	T	Significance of T
Percentage African American students	−.21188	−2.012	.0449
Substitute expenditures	−.02818	−.421	.6738
Age of school building	−.08514	−1.774	.0768
Percentage with advanced degrees	−.02317	−.287	.7745
Library books	.11765	1.797	.0731
School income	.20375	3.226	.0014
Instructional expenditures	.10259	1.602	.1099
Average teacher salary	−.27905	−3.594	.0004
Percentage African American teachers	.03758	.513	.6080
Average class size	−.02465	−.290	.7723
Student–Teacher ratio	−.01463	−.164	.8696
(Constant)		2.711	.0070

APPENDIX D:
SELECTED MULTIPLE REGRESSION STATISTICS
SCHOOL CHARACTERISTICS
BUSED MALE STUDENTS

Variables	Beta	T	Significance of T
Percentage African American students	−.15666	−.552	.5822
Average teacher salary	−.10299	−.688	.4934
Substitute expenditures	.06321	.472	.6385
Library books	.03660	.310	.7571
Age of school building	−.13399	−1.072	.2868
School income	.31942	−1.787	.0775
Instructional expenditures	.08440	.627	.5326
Percentage African American teachers	.13945	.795	.4291
Percentage with advanced degrees	−.01586	−.079	.9369
Student–Teacher ratio	−.04765	.228	.8199
Average class size	.13429	.576	.5660
(Constant)		.989	.3253

APPENDIX E:
Selected Multiple Regression Statistics
School Characteristics
All Bused Females

Variables	Beta	T	Significance of T
Percentage African American students	−.14233	−.608	.5455
Age of school building	.01342	.108	.9143
School income	.40253	2.483	.0156
Average teacher salary	−.09937	−.797	.4281
Substitute expenditures	.32611	2.150	.0353
Instructional expenditures	.21255	1.424	.1592
Library books	.34148	1.884	.0640
Percentage with advanced degrees	−.26105	−1.457	.1498
Percentage African American teachers	−.36363	−2.168	.0339
Average class size	.14346	.719	.4749
Student–Teacher ratio	−.23578	−1.128	.2635
(Constant)		.232	.8171

APPENDIX F:
Selected Multiple Regression Statistics
School Characteristics
All Bused Students

Variables	Beta	T	Significance of T
Percentage African American students	−.18103	−.993	.3224
Substitute expenditures	.10950	−1.156	.2495
Average teacher salary	−.05953	−.630	.5298
Age of school building	−.07789	−.935	.3510
Library books	.09000	1.000	.3186
School income	.30905	2.605	.0100
Instructional expenditures	.10249	1.029	.3052
Percentage African American teachers	−.04261	−.371	.7109
Percentage with advanced degrees	−.10980	−.831	.4070
Average class size	−.14011	.953	.3418
Student–Teacher ratio	.10535	−.716	.4753
(Constant)		.659	.5111

APPENDIX G:
Selected Multiple Regression Statistics
School Characteristics
All Non-Bused Males

Variables	Beta	T	Significance of T
Percentage African American students	1.15575	.860	.3917
Percentage African American teachers	.47450	.436	.6634
Percentage with advanced degrees	.17004	.219	.8269
Age of school building	.08616	.334	.7393
Average class size	−.04660	−.183	.8551
Substitute expenditures	−.28164	−.314	.7538
Instructional expenditures	.39008	.319	.6964
Student–Teacher ratio	.18017	.555	.5799
Average teacher salary	—	−.015	.9883
Library books	−.72849	−.302	.7631
(Constant)		1.143	.2555

APPENDIX H:
Selected Multiple Regression Statistics
School Characteristics
All Male Students

Variables	Beta	T	Significance of T
Percentage African American students	−.09137	−.322	.7484
Substitute expenditures	−.23750	−1.251	.2136
School income	.07532	.542	.5891
Percentage African American teachers	.29901	1.594	.1137
Age of school building	−.04932	.328	.7434
Average class size	−.43532	−2.371	.0194
Instructional expenditures	.01377	.068	.9458
Percentage with advanced degrees	.33099	1.445	.1511
Student–Teacher ratio	.37417	1.907	.0590
Average teacher salary	−.73440	−3.083	.0026
Library books	−.21258	−.705	.4825
(Constant)		1.143	.2555

APPENDIX I:
Selected Multiple Regression Statistics
School Characteristics
All Non-Bused Students

Variables	Beta	T	Significance of T
Percentage African American students	−.03628	−.165	.8687
Substitute expenditures	−.23659	−1.528	.1278
School income	.03419	−.387	.6988
Age of school building	.02303	.224	.8228
Percentage African American teachers	.25320	1.691	.0921
Average class size	−.26812	−1.976	.0492
Percentage with advanced degrees	.20395	1.221	.2233
Instructional expenditures	.10494	−.644	.5203
Student–Teacher ratio	.23351	1.636	.1031
Average teacher salary	−.61799	−3.185	.0016
Library books	−.10076	−.408	.6833
(Constant)		3.356	.0009

APPENDIX J:
Selected Multiple Regression Statistics
School Characteristics
All Chapter 1 Students

Variables	Beta	T	Significance of T
Percentage African American students	−.29532	−.991	.3259
Age of school building	.09088	.655	.5153
Average teacher salary	−.11341	−.782	.4375
Substitute expenditures	−1.6344	1.008	.3178
School income	.56854	2.723	.0085
Instructional expenditures	.20814	.993	.3246
Percentage African American teachers	−.36394	−1.859	.0681
Average class size	−.09232	−.428	.6700
Library books	−.32531	1.328	.1892
Percentage with advanced degrees	.20996	.844	.4020
Student–Teacher ratio	.02233	−.072	.9428
(Constant)		.082	.9348

APPENDIX K:
Selected Multiple Regression Statistics
School Characteristics
All Non Chapter 1 Students

Variables	Beta	T	Significance of T
Percentage African American students	−.22928	−1.881	.0608
Percentage with advanced degrees	−.01899	−.210	.8341
Age of school building	−.10348	−1.977	.0488
Substitute expenditures	−.09603	−1.199	.2313
Library books	.09158	1.357	.1756
School income	.15572	2.286	.0228
Instructional expenditures	.05056	.736	.4622
Percentage African American teachers	.12372	1.459	.1452
Average class size	—	.001	.9996
Student–Teacher ratio	—	−.033	.9735
Average teacher salary	.35589	−3.669	.0003
(Constant)		3.013	.0028

APPENDIX L:
Writing Assessment, Virginia 2005–2008

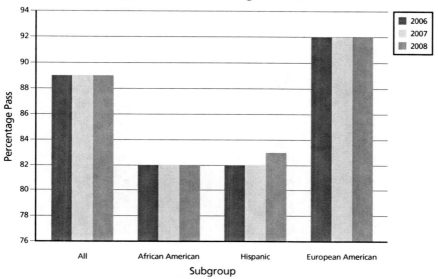

APPENDIX M:
History Assessment, Virginia 2006–2007

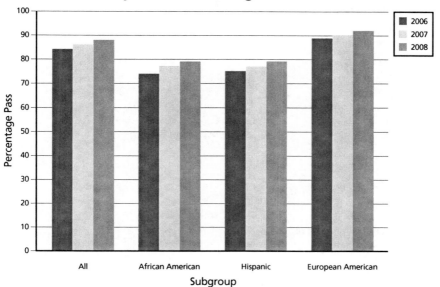

APPENDIX N:
Science Assessment, Virginia 2006–2008

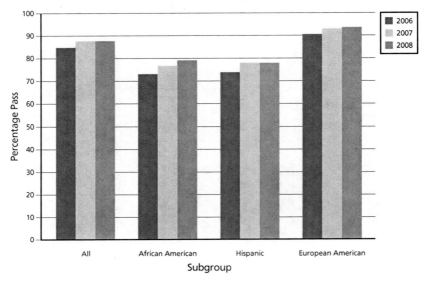

APPENDIX O:
Norfolk Elementary School Reading by Race, Ethnicity, and SES Achievement Gaps (2004–2007)

Elementary	2004	2005	2006	2007	Improvement
District					
All	73	78	82	83	1
African American	68	75	79	79	0
Asian	*	*	*	*	*
Hispanic	*	*	*	*	*
European American	85	84	89	90	1
Low Income	69	75	79	79	0
Non-low Income	82	84	88	90	2
State					
All	78	81	86	85	−1
African American	65	71	76	77	1
Asian	86	88	92	89	−3
Hispanic	70	74	80	72	−8
European American	84	86	90	90	0
Low Income	66	70	76	75	−2
Non-low Income	85	87	90	90	0

Source: The Eli and Edythe Broad Foundation: *Analysis of State Test Data* (2008)

APPENDIX P:
Norfolk High School Reading Achievement Gaps by Race, Ethnicity, and SES (2004–2007)

High	2004	2005	2006	2007	Improvement 2006–2007
District					
All	86	83	91	93	8
African American	81	77	88	92	11
Asian					
Hispanic					
European American	95	93	97	97	3
Low Income	82	—	90	90	8
Non-low Income	88	—	92	95	6
State					
All	89	88	90	94	4
African American	80	78	83	88	7
Asian	92	90	91	96	3
Hispanic	83	81	84	90	5
European American	93	92	94	96	3
Low Income	80	78	82	87	6
Non-low Income	91	90	92	96	4

Source: The Eli and Edythe Broad Foundation: *Analysis of State Test Data* (2008)

APPENDIX Q:
Norfolk Middle School Reading Achievement Gaps by Race, Ethnicity, and SES (2004–2007)

Middle	2004	2005	2006	2007	Improvement
District					
All	68	71	71	74	3
African American	61	64	67	69	2
Asian	*	*	*	*	*
Hispanic	*	*	*	*	*
European American	85	82	84	86	2
Low Income	62	65	67	69	2
Non-low Income	8	79	83	85	2
State					
All	72	76	81	82	1
African American	56	63	68	72	4
Asian	83	86	88	89	1
Hispanic	59	66	69	68	−1
European American	80	83	87	88	1
Low Income	54	61	67	69	1
Non-low Income	79	83	87	88	1

Source: The Eli and Edythe Broad Foundation: *Analysis of State Test Data* (2008).

APPENDIX R:
Norfolk Elementary School Mathematics Achievement Gaps by Race, Ethnicity, and SES (2004–2007)

Elementary	2004	2005	2006	2007	Improvement
District					
All	78	82	82	84	2
African American	74	78			
Asian					
Hispanic					
European American	89	90	91	91	0
Low Income	76	79	79	80	1
Non-low Income	85	87	90	91	1
State					
All	82	84	83	86	2
African American	71	74	73	77	3
Asian	92	92	91	93	2
Hispanic	77	77	75	77	3
European American	88	89	88	90	2
Low Income	72	74	73	76	3
Non-low Income	87	89	88	90	2

Source: The Eli and Edythe Broad Foundation: *Analysis of State Test Data* (2008).

APPENDIX S:
Norfolk Middle School Reading Achievement Gaps by Race, Ethnicity, and SES (2004–2007)

Middle	2004	2005	2006	2007	Improvement
District					
All	73	76	44	51	7
African American	67	70	38	44	6
Asian					
Hispanic					
European American	87	85	61	67	6
Low Income	70	71	38	44	7
Non-low Income	78	83	59	64	
State					
All	80	81	58	65	7
African American	67	67	41	50	9
Asian	93	93	76	82	6
Hispanic	73	73	45	52	7
European American	85	86	66	73	7
Low Income	67	67	41	50	9
Non-low Income	85	86	66	73	7

Source: The Eli and Edythe Broad Foundation: *Analysis of State Test Data* (2008).

APPENDIX T:
Norfolk High School Reading Achievement Gaps by Race, Ethnicity and SES (2004–2007)

High	2004	2005	2006	2007	Improvement
District					
All	80	81	79	82	0
African American	75	73	75	77	2
Asian					
Hispanic					
European American	89	91	87	89	–2
Low Income	79		76	77	–3
Non-low Income	81		82	86	3
State					
All	84	85	86	89	3
African American	71	75	76	81	5
Asian	92	93	92	95	1
Hispanic	76	79	79	84	4
European American	88	90	88	92	1
Low Income	75	77	78	81	3
Non-low Income	85	88	87	91	2

Source: The Eli and Edythe Broad Foundation: *Analysis of State Test Data* (2008).

APPENDIX U:
Norfolk English Achievement Gaps Pass Rates (2005–2008)

		Pass Rate		
Student Subgroup	Type	2005–2006	2006–2007	2007–2008
English				
All students	State	78	80	80
	NPS	84	85	87
Black	State	75	76	76
	NPS	73	76	78
Hispanic	State	76	80	82
	NPS	76	72	81
White	State	88	89	90
	NPS	89	90	91
Disabled	State	55	55	55
	NPS	64	62	67
Disadvantaged	State	74	75	75
	NPS	73	73	77
Limited English	State	54	71	77
	NPS	72	67	79

Source: Virginia Department of Education@www.doe.virginia.gov.- Norfolk City

APPENDIX V:
Norfolk Mathematics Achievement Gaps Pass Rates (2005–2008)

		Pass Rate		
Student Subgroup	Type	2005–2006	2006–2007	2007–2008
Mathematics				
All students	State	68	72	76
	NPS	76	80	84
Black	State	62	67	70
	NPS	62	68	73
Hispanic	State	72	76	80
	NPS	66	71	75
White	State	80	83	86
	NPS	81	85	88
Disabled	State	46	50	53
	NPS	53	58	65
Disadvantaged	State	62	66	71
	NPS	62	67	73
Limited English	State	75	72	81
	NPS	65	70	75

Source: Virginia Department of Education@www.doe.virginia.gov.- Norfolk City

APPENDIX W:
Norfolk Science Achievement Gaps Pass Rates (2005–2008)

Student Subgroup	Type	Pass Rate		
		2005–2006	2006–2007	2007–2008
Science				
All students	State	80	84	83
	NPS	85	88	88
Black	State	75	78	78
	NPS	73	77	79
Hispanic	State	82	86	84
	NPS	74	78	78
White	State	93	94	94
	NPS	91	93	94
Disabled	State	61	61	61
	NPS	65	67	69
Disadvantaged	State	75	79	78
	NPS	74	77	78
Limited English	State	71	70	78
	NPS	69	73	74

Source: Virginia Department of Education@www.doe.virginia.gov.- Norfolk City

APPENDIX X:
Norfolk Dropout Gaps (2005–2008)

Student Subgroup		2005–2006	2006–2007	2007–2008
Dropout Rate				
All students	Number	279	447	557
	Percentage	1.92	3.09	3.93
Female	Number	116	193	250
	Percentage	1.59	2.65	3.52
Male	Number	163	254	307
	Percentage	2.26	3.53	4.34
Black	Number	210	319	399
	Percentage	2.15	3.43	4.37
Hispanic	Number	—	13	21
	Percentage	58	3.07	4.74
White	Number	1.48	93	110
	Percentage		2.48	3.1

Source: Virginia Department of Education @www.doe.virginia.gov.

APPENDIX Y:
Grade 3 Reading and Mathematics Proficiency (2008)

	Reading proficiency	Math proficiency
All Students	78.0%	87.0%
African American	73.0%	83.0%
Hispanic	81.0%	86.0%
European American	87.0%	95.0%
Female	81.0%	88.0%
Male	75.0%	85.0%
Economically disadvantaged	74.0%	84.0%
English Language Learners	86.0%	92.0%
Students with disabilities	59.0%	68.0%

Source: Virginia Department of Education @www.doe.virginia.gov.

APPENDIX Z:
Grade 4 Reading and Mathematics Proficiency (2008)

	Reading proficiency	Math proficiency
All Students	84.0%	79.0%
African American	80.0%	75.0%
Hispanic	89.0%	85.0%
European American	91.0%	89.0%
Female	87.0%	81.0%
Male	81.0%	78.0%
Economically disadvantaged	80.0%	75.0%
English Language Learners	84.0%	86.0%
Students with disabilities	62.0%	57.0%

Source: Virginia Department of Education @www.doe.virginia.gov.

APPENDIX AA:
Grade 5 Reading and Mathematics Proficiency (2008)

	Reading proficiency	Math proficiency
All Students	87.0%	87.0%
African American	83.0%	84.0%
Hispanic	83.0%	88.0%
European American	93.0%	93.0%
Female	89.0%	89.0%
Male	84.0%	85.0%
Economically disadvantaged	83.0%	83.0%
English Language Learners	84.0%	82.0%
Students with disabilities	66.0%	66.0%

Source: Virginia Department of Education @www.doe.virginia.gov.

APPENDIX BB:
Grade 6 Reading and Mathematics Proficiency (2008)

	Reading proficiency	Math proficiency
All Students	75.0%	58.0%
African American	70.0%	50.0%
Hispanic	81.0%	68.0%
European American	84.0%	74.0%
Female	79.0%	59.0%
Male	71.0%	56.0%
Economically disadvantaged	71.0%	51.0%
English Language Learners	68.0%	57.0%
Students with disabilities	41.0%	35.0%

Source: Virginia Department of Education @www.doe.virginia.gov.

APPENDIX CC:
Grade 7 Reading and Math Proficiency (2008)

	Reading proficiency	Math proficiency
All Students	81.0%	53.0%
African American	76.0%	45.0%
Hispanic	83.0%	59.0%
European American	90.0%	67.0%
Female	83.0%	55.0%
Male	78.0%	51.0%
Economically disadvantaged	77.0%	47.0%
English Language Learners	78.0%	67.0%
Students with disabilities	52.0%	33.0%

Source: Virginia Department of Education @www.doe.virginia.gov.

APPENDIX DD:
Grade 8 Reading and Mathematics Proficiency (2008)

	Reading proficiency	Math proficiency
All Students	68.0%	66.0%
African American	61.0%	59.0%
Hispanic	67.0%	75.0%
European American	84.0%	81.0%
Female	70.0%	69.0%
Male	67.0%	62.0%
Economically disadvantaged	60.0%	60.0%
English Language Learners	56.0%	68.0%
Students with disabilities	39.0%	42.0%

Source: Virginia Department of Education @www.doe.virginia.gov.

APPENDIX EE:
High School Cohort Reading and Mathematics Proficiency (2008)

	Reading proficiency	Math proficiency
All Students	94.0%	65.0%
African American	92.0%	63.0%
Hispanic	92.0%	n.a.
European American	98.0%	n.a.
Female	94.0%	n.a.
Male	94.0%	64.0%
Economically disadvantaged	90.0%	63.0%
English Language Learners	61.0%	n.a.
Students with disabilities	73.0%	65.0%

Source: Virginia Department of Education @www.doe.virginia.gov.

APPENDIX FF:
Norfolk's Desegregation Plan

A. The desegregation plan was ordered by the Federal District Court into partial effect in 1970 and into full effect in 1971.
B. In general, the court ordered the following:
  1. *Full Faculty Desegregation*—with each school reflecting the existing race distribution at each level (elementary, junior and senior high).
  2. *Free Transportation*—Prior to 1971, school transportation was furnished by private municipal transit organizations, which were not under the direction of the school board. The company charged a fee for its services which was paid directly by the students. The court found that this practice constituted an unfair burden upon the plaintiffs and specified that the school board must provide free transportation as part of its desegregation plan. In the language accompanying this order, the court made it clear that it would not approve any plan which placed an unfair share of the burden of desegregation on African American children.
  3. *Student Assignment*—The court ordered the school board to prepare a student assignment plan to disestablish the racial identity of each school and to present that plan to the court for approval.

C. Student Assignment
    Elementary schools were arranged in pairs, triplets, and single atten-
    dance areas, with no school s assigned fewer than 40% of one race.
    Transportation was required for about one half of all students and
    was equally distributed between African American and European
    American neighborhoods.
D. Regulations
    The federal court required the school board to produce a school
    organization and student assignment plan that would eliminate the
    racial identity in each school. The court allowed the school board
    to devise the plan and to develop implementation policies. Gener-
    ally, the rules governing the school division's desegregation plan
    remained constant from 1970 to 1985. These plans were:
    1. School attendance boundaries will be not be drawn in such a
        manner as to assign students to racially identifiable schools. Ra-
        cially identifiable was defined as less than 30 % or more than
        70% minority or majority students.
    2. Attendance patterns were arranged in such a manner as to as-
        sign students to schools near their neighborhoods for a portion
        of the elementary grades. Single attendance zones were created
        wherever practical.

After a series of public debates, the chair of the Norfolk School Board
addressed the following issues and concerns with members of the board
and the public.

The Drawbacks of Busing

The practical drawbacks of mandatory busing have been amply discussed
as a result of hearings held by the school board on May 2, 1982. They include: loss of parental involvement and support; absorption of scarce resources that might otherwise be available for direct educational needs; loss
of large segment of community support; busing elimination of opportunities for educational advancement outside of normal school hours such as
extracurricular activities, administration of discipline and remedial tutor-
ing; disruption of communication between the home and school... loss of
middle class students; white and black to private schools and/or surrounding communities. With a consequent decline in desegregation; and last but
not least, the imposition of busing on some children but not others because
of the demographic makeup of the Norfolk neighborhoods. In the face of
such drawbacks, in a school system such Norfolk 's, which is legally deseg-

regated, a policy of massive cross-town at the elementary level should be supported only if the benefits to be gained are clear and compelling.

The Rationale for Busing

The three primary arguments in support of busing emerged from the public hearings held in May. (1) Bussing is needed to guarantee equal school resources. (2) Busing is needed to improve African American academic achievement. (3) Busing is desirable because it achieves desegregated schools.

Busing As a Guarantee of Equal School Resources

If mandatory busing were the only way to guarantee equal resource allocation for African American, then it would be unavoidable. I do not believe that it is necessary to guarantee equality of resources. The guarantee that I propose is that the school system report annually to the United States Magistrate for the United States Magistrate for the United States District Court for the Eastern District of Virginia. Such an annual report would detail the allocation of human and material resources devoted to the various elementary schools in the city of Norfolk.

Busing and Educational Achievement

Another compelling justification for continuation of massive cross-town busing might be present if busing held a clear promise of educational gain for African America children without detriment to others, provided that they policy itself did not result in a resegregated system and the loss of such benefit. If as I believe, the evidence shows, the policy itself is leading to a resegregated system, any benefit is not only speculative, but transitory.

Busing As a Means to End Desegregation

The primary potential justification for continuation of elementary school busing would be if it held reasonable prospects of assuring a stably desegregated system. We must not forget that the rationale behind the institution of such policy by the courts was to achieve desegregated school systems. Undoubtedly, the courts felt that such desegregated systems in themselves were good. It now appears, however that the policy is counterproductive to a stably desegregated school system.

The choice before us is not a metropolitan plan but a plan for massive cross-town busing in Norfolk while adjacent residential communities rely on buses to serve only neighborhood elementary schools. If the decision before us concerned a plan that covered the entire metropolitan area making up one community, the considerations at this point might be different. We must deal with the situation as it is and not as one might wish it to be.

Many proponents of busing maintain that the school system has no right to take into account the reactions of white parents to busing and the refusal of such parents to submit their children to mandatory busing. Such proponents maintain that such white reactions reflects racism and it I not busing to which such whites object, but to going to school with blacks.
While there may be such sentiment in a few, I do not feel that that is the motivation of the vast majority of whites.

The effect of the institution of busing in Norfolk is history. The more relevant question is what effect will continued busing have on resegregation of the Norfolk School system. And what effect will the adoption of neighborhood schools have on stemming the outflow of middle class black and white students from the schools.

Dilemma

In the face of such projections, the dilemma before us is clearly posed. If we do nothing, in all probability, the Norfolk School System will resegregate to the point where all or nearly all of our schools will be racially identifiable. The middle class will have fled the school system and the children, black and white, who are left with the poorest, most powerless, both economically and politically, segment of our society.

(Norfolk School Board Meeting, January 23, 1983.)

ABOUT THE AUTHORS

C. Kent McGuire is the Dean of the College of Education at Temple University and Professor of Educational Leadership and Policy Studies. He also served with the U.S. Department of Education as Assistant Secretary of Education for the Office of Education Research and Improvement. Additionally, he held posts with the Pew Charitable Trust and Eli Lily Endowment and was senior vice president at the Manpower Demonstration Research Corporation, where his responsibilities included leadership of the education, children and youth division. The author's research interests focus on the areas of education administration and policy, and organizational change. He has been involved in a number of evaluation research initiatives on comprehensive school reform, education finance, and school improvement.

Vivian Ikpa is an Associate Professor of Educational Leadership and Policy Studies at Temple University. She has held positions as a policy analyst at the United States Department of Education; Director of the Center for Education Policy Research, Longwood, Florida; K–12 classroom teacher. She has also contributed to numerous research initiatives related to education policy and student performance. Her research continues to examine the impact of changes in selected school characteristics on the achievement gap between disadvantaged and non-disadvantaged children.

INDEX

Page numbers followed by *t, f, a* in *italics* refer to tables, figures, and appendices respectively.

Narrowing the Achievement Gap in a (Re)Segregated Urban School District, pages 173–182
Copyright © 2009 by Information Age Publishing

LaVergne, TN USA
23 October 2009
161893LV00002B/49/P

9 781607 522218